RENCH HAS WRITTEN an honest and gripping account of uncontrolled Bipolar Disorder and its poignant and potentially catastrophic consequences in a marriage. She sheds harsh light on what this mental illness can be, but gives hope to those people and their families who receive this diagnosis.

—Dorothy S. Brown
(Living with Bipolar for 50 years)

THE ROLLER COASTER RIDE is a 'must read' for anyone living with or around a person with this illness. Fascinating and informative for the layman, yet clinical enough to keep the interest of the mental health professional, Ms. Rench has come up with another winner.

—Lucie Duvall
(Retired 24 year veteran law enforcement officer)

I FEEL LIKE I JUST READ MY OWN LIFE STORY! What a relief to know I'm not the only person struggling with a family member with this disorder. It certainly helps to understand the ripple effect this has on the lives of people you love.

—Beje Beasley

MS. RENCH'S GRIPPING BOOK takes us on a ride through a life of euphoria and despair in Part 1, then provides us with valuable, easily understandable resources to help cope with bipolar and other mental illnesses in Part 2. The Roller Coaster Ride is a must read for anyone who loves or is living with a person with bipolar.—

—Barbara Hartford,
(Former Mental Health Administrator)

—THE ROLLER COASTER RIDE—

Bipolar Disorder

by

Janice Bingham Rench

—DISCLAIMER—

THE *ROLLER COASTER RIDE* REPRESENTS THE EXPERIENCES of the author, as well as those of many other individuals who love someone with bipolar disorder. Without their willingness to share their experiences, there would be no story to tell.

Although some parts of this story have been loosely based on true events, the author wishes to state that this story is a work of fiction. The characters, names, and places in this book are a blend of other people's experiences and the author's imagination.

Library of Congress Control Number: Pending

Rench, Janice Bingham

Includes index.

ISBN: 1456348736

1. The Roller Coaster Ride

Cover and Book Design by Ken Bingham

Web Page design and management by John Kohler

JANICE BINGHAM RENCH
860 WORCESTER RD.
FRAMINGHAM, MA 01702

(e-mail) — JBR@janicerench.com
(web site) — http://janicerench.com/
(blog)   — http://janicerench.blogspot.com
(Tel.)   — 508-309-0948

Printed in The United States

—DEDICATION—

THIS BOOK IS DEDICATED TO MY MOTHER
—ELIZABETH M. PRENTISS—
AND TO ALL THOSE WHO STRUGGLE
WITH THE DEPTHS OF HELL AND THE HEIGHTS OF HEAVEN.

—The world breaks everyone and afterward many are strong in the broken places.— *From "A Farewell to Arms" by Ernest Hemingway.*

—ACKNOWLEDGMENTS—

I T IS WITH ENORMOUS PLEASURE AND PRIDE THAT I SHARE *The Roller Coaster Ride* with you, the reader. This writing journey would not have been possible without the ongoing support and assistance from my family and friends.

Thank you to Caren Kaplan, Laura Ter Keurst, Chris Parli, Bonnie Dalton, and Kathy Perry for reading the manuscript in its earliest stages. Your comments were very helpful as the book began to develop.

Thank you, Steffanie and Tepe, for all of your love and support during this endeavor. Special thank you to John Kohler for the design and management of the web page and all other technical issues. Special gratitude goes to Elizabeth, and Tom, and their spouses. To Richard Bingham who at the last hour took time to read the manuscript and offered valuable editing and suggestions·

A huge thank-you goes to my special friend, Dotti, for your thoughtful comments and editing. Thank you also to Megan Northrup, typist, who had the daunting task of sifting through many stacks of handwritten notes.

Finally, I want to acknowledge the two people who saw this manuscript to the end with me. If not for them it might be still sitting on my desk. Ken Bingham, I am so grateful for your insightful way of asking the tough questions and keeping me motivated to keep writing, along with numerous hours of printing, reading and editing. To Sally Leffingwell who was in on the process from the beginning and never waivered with her support and encouragement. Hours of reading and rereading, and the writing and rewriting that she endured, all with good humor. Words alone can not express, to both of you, my gratitude and indebtedness for your generous support, and your belief that this story was worth writing.

Janice Bingham Rench, June 2010

—CONTENTS—

CONTENTS *(Cont.)*

PART TWO

—INTRODUCTION—

The *Roller Coaster Ride* is a book written for people who love someone with bipolar disorder. The purpose of this book is to increase understanding, raise awareness, and give hope to those involved with this disorder, so that more positive endings can be accomplished.

What causes this illness? Is there a cure? How do I find the best treatment? What medications are available? This book will answer these very important questions.

The *Roller Coaster Ride* is written in two parts. Part One tells the fictional story of Sam and Marian, who meet and fall in love while Sam is in a manic high. Through the events in the story, the reader will gain an understanding of the many challenges associated with bipolar disorder. This story is based on my own personal experiences, as well as on many different stories I have heard during my years of working as a counselor.

Part Two will inform the reader about bipolar disorder: the symptoms of the illness, effective interventions to use with loved ones, and what treatment options are available. Topics such as hospitalization, medications, how to handle manic aggression, and the risk of suicide will be discussed. Frequently-asked questions and their answers are also included.

Even though bipolar disorder is caused by a malfunctioning of the brain, society has a long way to go toward eliminating the stigma associated with mental disorders. In addition to informing the reader, it is my goal to demystify mental illness and the stigma attached to it.

Bipolar disorder presents many challenges, not only to the people who have the disorder, but also to the people who love them. I hope *The Roller Coaster Ride* promotes a better understanding of this illness, and provides support to those who are directly affected by it.

PART ONE

—Chapter 1—

THE BEGINNING OF THE END
1989

SOME OF THE MOST SIGNIFICANT THOUGHTS CAN OCCUR
somewhere between dawn and waking. It is then that
nature allows the mind to make a connection between con-
scious and unconscious thinking ... where you are, who you
are, and the recognition of familiar surroundings. This was
the state that Marian was in when she reached over to the
left side of the bed to touch the man she loved.

She searched with her hand, slowly patting the mattress,
expecting to feel the familiar contours of his body. Instead,
with a shiver, she realized she was alone. Her eyes confirmed
what her mind had not yet comprehended ... the reality
that Sam was not there. She continued to pat the other side
of the bed as if, by that very act, she could change the reality
of the moment and he would appear.

Finally, leaning on her side, she grabbed his pillow and
hugged it close to her chest. She didn't cry ... her tears had
long ago dried up. With his pillow in her arms, she rocked
back and forth as she remembered the night before.

Although he had been hurried in his desire and caresses,
he had been very tender and had prolonged his own pleasure
while giving to her.

"Oh Marian, I love you," he had murmured as he buried
his face in her neck. "I couldn't exist without you."

Her final memories of last night were his words and of

1

looking at the numbers on the clock: 1:35 a.m. She had continued to lie in his arms until sleep overtook her.

Now, with a quickening heartbeat, she pulled the pillow away from her face to look at the clock. She looked once, and then again—5:15 a.m. She had a sickening sense that Sam had never gone to sleep the night before. Just then, she heard sounds of banging, scraping, and clanging coming from the driveway.

Walking from the bed to the window, she looked down to the front yard. To the right was the driveway, running from the street toward the back of the house where the garage sat. What she saw prompted her to go to the laundry room at the back of the house to see the rest of the driveway. Looking out the laundry room window, she raised her hand and covered her mouth to silence the scream in her throat. What a startling sight to behold. It was too much to comprehend all at once.

Along both sides of the driveway, there were tables piled high with household items from the house and basement. Antiques were mixed in with cheap items, rare books were piled high beside contemporary paper-backs. Some of the items were from a family legacy, carefully preserved and passed down for generations. It was surreal looking down into her yard. There before her was a lifetime of memories, hopes, and dreams, all on display. The man who had spent eighteen years helping her acquire these possessions was now putting them up for sale. Marian felt as though she was exposed, naked for anyone and everyone to touch and examine. The image of the driveway opened a floodgate of emotions ... laughter first, then uncontrollable tears, sobbing, and trembling.

Marian stood motionless at the window for a long time. It was now almost 7:00. Soon flea-market early-birds would descend upon her yard. Knowing Sam as she did, she knew he would enjoy the bartering one goes through during a sale. That would be a challenge for him: who would get what item and at what cost.

Finally, Marian regained control and quickly headed toward the bathroom. She splashed cold water on her face, ran her fingers through her hair, and brushed her teeth before putting on clothes from the day before. As she started to leave the bathroom, she turned and opened the cabinet over the sink. Behind Sam's shaving kit was his familiar plastic medicine bottle. She reached to grab it and realized it was empty. It hadn't been refilled in over a month. With anger, she threw the bottle into the sink and watched as it bounced from side to side.

Going back to the bedroom, she noticed that a truck had already pulled up in front of the house. She heard Sam's voice, but was unable to hear exactly what he was saying. As she continued to look out the window, her attention was drawn to something she saw out of the corner of her eye. Her Victorian settee was being carried out of the house.

Marian's mind went back to the day she bought that settee. Victorian furniture hadn't been part of Marian's interior design until one day, while shopping for fabric at Frederick's Upholstery Store, she saw it. It had meticulous hand-carving, and the walnut wood had a soft luster. Although the seat and back were missing its upholstery, Marian knew just the fabric she would choose: a pink, old-fashioned rose pattern. She visualized this prized piece displayed in the corner of her living room. Indulging herself was something she seldom did, but since she had saved some money of her own, Marian decided to purchase it. She had been so excited about this beautiful piece of functional art and the pleasure it would bring. Now Sam was totally oblivious to her feelings. Marian watched as the precious settee was tied on the back of the truck and covered with a sheet.

Marian yelled down the stairs. "Sam, Sam, come here!"

"What do you want? Go back to bed, it's still early," Sam responded.

"What are you doing? We need to talk."

Sam waved his fist in the air and yelled angrily, "This is not your business. Go back to bed."

"Sam, it is my business," Marian exclaimed frantically. "That is my settee. Please don't sell it. It's worth over thirteen-hundred dollars and you know how much I love it."

"We don't need this stuff. We have too much stuff. This house is too big for only two people. Some people don't even have a house." His voice was loud and angry.

Just a few hours earlier, he had been physically and emotionally connected to her. Yet, within a short amount of time, he had been able to disconnect from her and find some disjointed meaning in the activity of the moment. He had become consumed by it.

Marian watched as the truck with the precious settee pulled away from the house. With a feeling of panic, she rushed outdoors. Desperate to salvage all that she could, she ran from table to table, gathering as many keepsakes as she could hold in her arms.

From the garage, Sam ran up to her and they stood glaring at each other. The look between them was antagonistic, and a few words said it all.

"What are you doing with those things?" Sam yelled.

"These are my things. It isn't too late to stop what is happening here. You need to go back on your medication."

"No, I am through taking medicine. I like this feeling, so get out of here and leave me alone."

At that moment, items began tumbling from her arms onto the pavement. The sounds of glass breaking and books hitting the pavement with a thud shook Marian. She caught a glimpse of people standing silently, staring at her and Sam in utter disbelief. She left the scene that was engulfing her, running from the driveway and up the back stairs. In the meantime, Sam had begun to bargain with the many customers who congregated around the tables. He was animated and enthralled by his audience.

Marian made her way to the bedroom and collapsed on the bed. Sounds of car motors, laughter, and talking slowly drifted around her as she remembered what had brought her to this day.

She continued to lie on the bed while memories faded to black and white. She saw the past like it was an old movie, one in which she cried inconsolably in the final scene. The tears of love, heartbreak, and devastation collided while the voices and laughter continued in the background.

—Chapter 2—

FLASHBACK 1971

Marian pulled into the driveway after work and quickly picked up the mail on her way into the house. Her mind was on overload. Between working part-time and raising three children with the help of her ex-husband, she had a heavy schedule.

She decided to check her mail and take a short rest before fixing dinner. Marian was happy to see an envelope from her good friend, Sue, that was mixed in with the usual assortment of bills and ads. She quickly opened it, her curiosity piqued.

Marian,
I'm having a small get-together Friday eve ... just a casual gathering with plenty of food and good conversation. Would love to have you come. Please don't say you're too busy!!
Love, Sue

Marian sighed as she thought about her weekly schedule. Finding time for social events was not necessarily a high priority. Even though she loved spending time with Sue, she was tired of dinner dates and idle conversation. However, as the week-end approached, Marian changed her mind. Knowing that her kids had plans to be with their dad, she decided to go for dinner and then leave early.

When Friday evening arrived, Marian was already second-guessing her decision. She arrived at Sue's house feeling rather bored. However, when Sue answered the door, Marian greeted her with a smile and an enthusiastic hug. Marian's chestnut-brown hair was pulled back from her face, highlighting her high cheekbones and olive skin. Her lavender jersey dress skimmed over her slender body and accented her hips as she moved from the front door into the living room. Greeting those she knew and introducing herself to others, she quickly got caught up in the laughter and noisy chatter of her surroundings.

Marian was busy mingling with the guests when she felt a tap on her shoulder. Marian turned to see Sue standing behind her.

"Marian, I'd like you to meet a friend of mine from Chicago. Sam is here on business for a couple of days."

Marian held out her hand to Sam, noticing that their handshake lasted longer than usual. As Marian looked at his well-trimmed beard, tailored suit, and spit-shined shoes, she became fixated by his aquamarine eyes that sparkled as he looked at her.

She immediately felt drawn to him and could barely get the words out of her dry mouth; "Nice to meet you, Sam. I'm Marian. Welcome to Pennsylvania." She began to wonder if this evening would be more interesting than she expected.

She watched Sam as he circulated around the room, engaging in animated conversation with a zeal she had never witnessed before. He was definitely in command of the evening and seemed to be enjoying every minute of it. His openness and interest in what others were saying made him the most magnetic person in the room. Marian was mesmerized. She had never met anyone like Sam, and became engrossed by the way he interacted with the other guests. She was pleased to see that he kept glancing in her direction.

The evening went well. There was easy conversation, good food, and plenty of fine wine. Marian didn't want it to end. As people began saying their good-byes, Sam approached her. He gently put his hand on the small of her back and guided her to a quiet corner of the room.

"We haven't had much of a chance to visit, Marian. I'd really like to get to know you better. Would you like to go somewhere for a drink?"

Marian knew she wanted to know more about Sam, and yet she wasn't sure it was a smart idea to be alone with this charming man. After all, she didn't really know anything about him. She looked around the room until she saw Sue.

"Sam, excuse me for a moment. I want to thank Sue for a wonderful evening."

"Sure, I'll wait right here."

Marian hastily walked to the far corner of the room and whispered in Sue's ear. "Sam wants to meet me for a drink. How well do you know him? Do you think it's safe to be alone in a bar with him?" As soon as she asked that last question, she thought of how silly it must have sounded to Sue.

"Marian, he is a good friend. He comes here on business pretty often, and to my knowledge, he isn't a mass murderer or a 'Jack The Ripper' type." She laughed as she put her arm around Marian's shoulder. "Go for it, my friend. I think you'll really enjoy getting to know him."

Marian was thrilled to get Sue's approval. She was on Cloud Nine as she joined Sam.

"I'd love to have a drink with you. Where are you staying?" Sam told her the name of the hotel.

"That's on my way home. No sense calling a cab. You can ride back to the hotel with me, then we can stop at the hotel bar for a nightcap," Marian suggested.

When they arrived, Marian was glad to see that the bar wasn't too crowded. Sam pointed to a booth along the back wall … a perfect place for quiet conversation. Sam was just as fascinating as he had been at the party, and Marian listened intently as he went from one subject to another.

"Why doesn't Pennsylvania have men like Sam? I've been waiting all my life to meet someone like him," she thought wistfully.

As the waitress brought their second drink, Sam reached over and took her hand. As he continued talking, Marian thought about how long it had been since a man had touched her with such tenderness.

When Sam finished the last sip of his drink, he winked at her. "How about coming to my room, Marian?"

He put his arm around her as they walked slowly to his hotel room. Marian felt as though she was in a wonderful dream.

Their strong desire for one another overwhelmed both of them, leaving Marian deliriously happy as she rested in Sam's arms the next morning. When he postponed his plans to return home that day, Marian was elated. For the rest of the week-end, they stayed up late, talked endlessly, and made love freely. For Marian, what started out as a casual dinner with friends somehow ended up as a romantic week-end.

As Sam began packing for his flight back to Chicago, he turned to Marian. "There's something you need to know. I have a son, George. He's a great kid."

Marian took a deep breath as she felt her mood plunge.

"And do you also have a wife waiting for you in Chicago?"

"Her name is Penny, but don't worry about her. We're separated and our divorce proceedings will be over soon." Sam seemed so nonchalant as he told her about his family.

"What am I doing, getting involved with a married man?" she thought. She knew this wasn't a wise thing to do, but the memories of the wonderful week-end blocked out the nagging doubts in her mind.

Saying good-bye to Sam at the airport was difficult for her. As Sam went back to Chicago, Marian stayed behind to continue her life as before ... but not really. Her life would never again be the same. He called every day, talking about how much he missed her, and Marian found herself waiting eagerly for his next phone call. Getting to know Sam was the best thing that had happened to her in a long time.

When Sam finally phoned to say his divorce papers had been signed, she was relieved. His voice was filled with excitement, and Marian got swept up in their talk about the future.

"Now you can move to Chicago and we can finally be together," he exclaimed.

"Sam, I want that more than anything. But you know I have to think of my family first. If I move to Chicago, my kids and I will have some big decisions to make. Would they come to Chicago with me or what?" Marian's head was spinning with everything she needed to think about. "I just don't know if this is the right thing for me to do."

"Marian, we're soul-mates. We should be together for

the rest of our lives." Although Sam was five hundred miles away, he was still the most persuasive, confident man Marian had ever met.

Finally Sam's loving, hypnotic words convinced her they should be together. She was weary of her humdrum life … the same boring routine every day. More importantly, she admitted to herself that she loved this man who had swept into her life just a few short months ago. Life with Sam was too enticing to pass up. But what about her kids?

When she and her husband divorced two years earlier, it had been a very difficult time for her children. Fifteen-year-old Edward had always been a serious child. Since the divorce, he had worried a lot about how his dad was getting along. Although it had never been easy for him to talk about his feelings, that seemed to be even harder for him now.

Charles, the thirteen-year-old, had a quick wit and an infectious grin. He never took anything too seriously, not even his school work. He was a busy teenager who always seemed to be involved in some kind of activity.

Marian's thoughts then turned to her daughter. As a ten-year-old, Susan loved to be in the middle of everything her brothers were doing, but she was shy and timid when they weren't around. Frilly dresses and bows were not her style; she was most comfortable wearing jeans and sneakers. Marian remembered how quiet Susan had been when she was told about her parents' divorce.

A few weeks later, Marian called Sam to fill him in on the latest developments.

"I've been really worried about what the move to Chicago would mean for my kids, Sam. Their dad and I have talked to them for hours and hours, and we've had several sessions with a family counselor. I think everything is finally beginning to fall into place."

"And"… Sam asked impatiently.

"Well, the kids and their dad have always been close. I can't begin to tell you what a loving, devoted father he is. Since the divorce, they've spent lots of time with him, so we've decided it will be best if the kids stay with him here in Pennsylvania. I think it would be hard for them to move to a new city, Sam. They would really miss their dad and all of their friends. I'm sure it would be hard for them to adjust to a new school, too. Even though I can't imagine being away from them, we all agree this is the best plan."

Sam was elated. "Don't worry about a thing, Marian. Everything will work out great. I'm going to start making plans for your move right now. Have everything packed by next week-end. I'll come to pick you up on Saturday."

Marian started to say, "But Sam, that's only 5 days away," but before she could get the words out, she heard a click on the other end of the line. Excited and yet apprehensive, Marian began to pack her belongings and take care of last-minute business.

She was surprised, then, to hear Sam's voice when she answered her phone on Thursday morning.

"Marian, I've decided to leave early. I've stopped along the way to get a haircut and grab some breakfast. I should be at your house by midnight."

"I thought you were coming on Saturday…you'll be here tonight?"

Marian thought about the packing and errands she still needed to do. "You have a long drive ahead of you, Sam. Why don't you stop at a motel along the way and get some rest?"

"I don't need rest, Marian. The only thing I need is you." The flattery overwhelmed her; she could barely speak.

Sam arrived before midnight and immediately began loading Marian's suitcases in the car.

"I thought we could start back to Chicago right away," he said.

"Slow down, Sam. Before we leave, I want you to meet my kids. I promised them we'd spend the week-end together. Saying goodbye to them is going to be so hard." Marian's eyes began to flood with tears.

"Well, I guess that'll be OK. After all, we have the rest of our lives to be together." When the time finally came to leave for Chicago, Marian questioned whether she was doing the right thing. Pangs of doubt were mixed with feelings of excitement, but Sam was as persuasive as always. He assured her they would come back to Pennsylvania in a few weeks to see her kids.

In such a short period of time, Marian's life had taken a dramatic turn. Even though her inner voice sent out warnings—"Be careful, be cautious, take it slow"—she ignored them. She managed to ignore other red flags as well. The emotional and physical tugs she experienced when she was with Sam took center stage, leaving no time for self-examination.

When Sam held out his hand, Marian willingly took it. Together, they boarded what felt like a roller coaster ride: in full motion at top speed. It took many more years before Marian learned that this ride with Sam was too wild, too risky, and too exhilarating for her to hold on to him ... or to herself.

—Chapter 3—

A Crack In The Dream

As she rode from pennsylvania to chicago with Sam, Marian was filled with excitement and the expectation of having a "and they lived happily ever after" life with him. She thought of Sue's party, thinking how different her life had become because of that evening.

The next few months were a whirlwind. Living with Sam was everything she had hoped for. "Is this too good to be true," she would ask herself, but then would quickly dismiss the thought. She kept reassuring herself this was the relationship she wanted and deserved.

One day, while unpacking some of Sam's books, she noticed that many of them were psychology books. Inside the front covers, page numbers were written in red. As Marian turned to those pages, the subject matter was all the same: manic-depression[1], symptoms of depression, and mood disorders. Definitions and medications were highlighted with red underlining. She was curious about why he was interested in these topics. Marian was fairly certain that Sam was probably trying to diagnose someone. But who?

She knew that Sam was a well-educated man, so Marian assumed the psychology books were ones he had saved from his college days. As she kept busy with the routine of their

---

1 *At the time of the story, manic-depression was the term used for bipolar disorder.*

daily lives, she would occasionally think of the psychology books.

It wasn't long after the discovery of the books that Marian began to see changes in Sam's behavior. When she had first moved to Chicago, she had noticed Sam's high energy level even though he had been getting very little sleep. Now, just a few weeks later, he had trouble getting out of bed to go to work. Once so warmly communicative and confident, he began to talk less and less. Any effort to engage him in the simplest conversation was met with a short answer or just a simple shrug of his shoulders. They used to love spending their evenings together. They would have lengthy discussions about books they had read, listen to classical music while curled up together on the couch, or take long walks after dinner. But now Sam only wanted to sit in front of the television, silent and despondent. Passionate lovemaking changed into deep sighs as he turned away from her. It was obvious that something was terribly wrong. Sam seemed so depressed. However, this was different from any kind of depression she had ever witnessed.

One afternoon, Marian decided to bring up the subject. "Sam, you seem to be feeling kind of low. What's wrong? Are you unhappy that I'm here?"

"Everything's fine, Marian." Sam sat down in his recliner and began looking out the front window.

"You'll tell me if something is wrong, won't you, Sam?"

He nodded slightly in her direction. "I'm okay. You don't need to worry."

Time passed as Marian waited for Sam's mood to improve. She wanted to talk to him about so many things. She had suggested they go to Iowa so she could meet his family, but he seemed apprehensive at the thought of making that trip. They had also talked about bringing the kids to Chicago to spend a few days, but Sam hadn't made any arrangements for their visit. "And why isn't he sending any child support payments?" she wondered.

Marian kept hoping that Sam's erratic behavior was just the result of learning to live together as a couple. His inconsistent moods continued, however. He could be agitated, irritable, and unable to make the smallest decisions. Then suddenly, without explanation, he would become playful, happy, and full of grandiose thinking. Life with Sam was certainly unpredictable.

If Marian told him news about her day as soon as he came home from work, he would sometimes angrily say, "Can't you give me a chance to relax? Do you have to hit me with this as soon as I walk in the door?" And yet, if she waited until dinner was over to share the day's news, he would often become upset and start yelling, "Why didn't you tell me this sooner?"

Even when things appeared to be going smoothly, it wasn't unusual for Sam to have an emotional outburst over some minor incident. At first Marian overlooked the outbursts and tried to smooth things over, but as time went on, her patience wore thin. Finally, after an evening of Sam's relentless ranting, Marian found the courage to confront his behavior.

"Sam, what's going on with you? Are things all right at work?"

"Everything would be fine if you'd just stop asking me so many questions," he snapped.

"You're either angry or silent, Sam, and there never

seems to be a good time to talk about decisions we need to make."

"What do we need to talk about?"

Marian could hear the anxiety in his voice. "I don't care how upset he is," she thought. "I've been patient long enough. It's time for him to snap out of this."

Marian continued. "We need to make reservations to go to Pennsylvania to see my kids."

Sam's face went blank. "What are you talking about?"

"Remember, you promised that we would go back to see them, and we only have three weeks to make plans. Are we flying? Driving? What?"

"Cancel the trip. We don't need to be there."

"I made a promise to my kids, but even more than that, I want to be there." Each word became louder. "You promised you would never stand between me and my kids. You promised … you promised!" With each word, she banged her fist on the table, her agitated voice vibrating throughout the room. Sam sat silently, staring at his plate of food.

"You don't have to go, but I am," Marian shouted. Sobbing, she ran to the bedroom and slammed the door. She couldn't believe Sam would even think of going back on his promise. When he came in to get ready for bed, neither of them spoke.

The next morning, Marian stayed in bed until after Sam left for work. When she finally went into the kitchen, she found a note on the table:

We will drive back.
Sam

While she fixed breakfast, she thought about last night's testy conversation. She reminded herself that Sam had been under a lot of pressure at work. Maybe that has been the cause of his moody behavior. Marian decided she just needed to be more patient and understanding. She began leafing through her recipe book, hoping a nice dinner tonight would help clear the air.

After washing the breakfast dishes, she vacuumed the living room rug and began tidying up. As she dusted the bookcase, Marian noticed the psychology books on the shelf. She wondered if there was any information in those books that would help her understand Sam a little better. She was tempted to look through some of them, but talked herself out of it. For now, she just wanted to think about the upcoming trip to see her children.

She desperately missed being with her kids. When Marian had moved to Chicago to be with Sam, she had known her children would be with a great dad.

Still, she couldn't wait to be in Pennsylvania again to see with her own eyes that everything was, in fact, going smoothly.

The days leading up to the trip seemed to pass slowly for Marian as she organized everything they needed to take. On the morning she and Sam were leaving on their trip, Marian woke up at 4:30, filled with excitement at the thought of seeing her kids. She wasn't surprised to see that Sam was already up. For the last two weeks, his nights had been restless and he hadn't been getting much sleep. She noticed he had already showered and gotten dressed.

"I'll be ready soon," Marian said as she climbed out of bed.

"Take your time … it's still early. Oh, and don't bother fixing breakfast, Marian. There will be plenty of places along the way where we can stop to eat."

When Marian came downstairs, Sam was waiting patiently at the kitchen table, finishing a cup of coffee. She rolled their suitcases outside and left them by the front door. As she walked back past the table, he grabbed her hand and playfully pulled her onto his lap. He nestled his lips against her neck and whispered, "Do you want to go back to bed for a while?"

Marian giggled and ruffled his hair. "Can I take a rain check on your offer?" she asked. Sam had been so moody lately, so Marian was relieved when he took her response in stride.

"Okay, then. Let's get the suitcases loaded in the car," he replied.

As they drove out of the city, the sunrise over Lake Michigan was breathtaking. The reflection on the water left streaks of red, yellow, and orange … just like beautiful satin ribbons. Country music was playing on the car radio, and they both sang in harmony, laughing and making up words as they went along. Sam talked endlessly: about the weather, where he wanted to take the kids, about the newest sculpture at Penn State University. He skipped from subject to subject without giving Marian time to respond.

When they lost the reception on the music station, Sam found a religious program on the radio that sent him into a frenzy that both frightened and amused Marian. He started yelling and ranting as if the preacher on the radio could hear him. For the first time, he told Marian about his religious beliefs and experiences. He talked about spiritualism, reincarnation, the spirits of deceased people, and the many times he felt that God had spoken to him. He sounded very knowledgeable as he quoted authors and talked about references from many different books. Whenever Marian began to express her own opinions, Sam started pontificating. When he finally ran out of energy, there was silence during the rest of the trip.

Marian was relieved when they arrived at the hotel earlier than planned. After checking into their room and unpacking, Marian couldn't wait to see her kids. When she and Sam pulled into the driveway to pick them up, the front door flew open and out ran Charles and Susan. Marian hardly had time to get out of the car before Charles ran into her outstretched arms.

"Charles! I've missed you so much," she exclaimed as she gave him a big hug and kiss. Keeping one arm around Charles, Marian engulfed Susan in an embrace with her other arm. They stood, rocking back and forth in a big bear hug. It felt wonderful to have her arms around them again.

Then Edward came out of the house, walking slowly with his head down. Marian held out her arms. There was a moment of hesitation, but finally Edward allowed his mom to give him a big hug as well.

"Edward, you can't imagine how great it is to see you. I love you so much."

"Ah, Mom," was the only thing Edward said. Even through his teenage awkwardness, she could tell that he was enjoying the attention.

The laughter and tears of joy seemed to ease the nervousness everyone was feeling, and Marian was ecstatic to see her children looking healthy and happy.

During dinner, Sam talked excitedly about the many plans he had for the week-end. The kids were delighted and added their own ideas, while Marian reminded everyone they only had a few days to accomplish all they wanted to do. And so the fun-filled week-end began.

Sam actively participated in all of the activities, and the kids treated him like a big brother instead of a father figure. They were on the go from early morning until late at night. The kids loved it ... Marian was exhausted but happy...and Sam had boundless energy left over at the end of each long day.

During dinner on their last evening together, everyone was excited as plans were made for the kids' trip to Chicago during their school vacation. Although these plans made the separation easier, Marian had to try hard to hold herself together as they said their good-byes later that night. She wondered if she would ever get used to being away from her kids.

—Chapter 4—

The Walmart Splurge

SAM WAS UP BRIGHT AND EARLY THE FOLLOWING MORN-
ING, ready to start the trip home. As Marian got dressed
and finished packing the last of her belongings, she was sad
that the visit with her kids was over. The week-end had been
wonderful, and she had loved every minute of it.

Even though Marian was exceptionally quiet and with-
drawn, Sam didn't really pay attention to her mood. He was
in his own little world, filled with energy and enthusiasm.

After eating breakfast at a small roadside cafe, Sam
announced, "I want to stop at Walmart to pick up a few
things."

"We don't really need anything, Sam. Let's just keep driving. I'm tired and want to get home."

"We have plenty of time, Marian. It's a beautiful day, so
let's make the most of it."

"Okay, Sam, do your shopping. I'll wait in the car for
you. But please ... don't take too long. We have a long trip
ahead of us."

Sam pulled into the store's parking lot. "I'll be back
soon," he promised.

Marian waited and waited for Sam to reappear. When he
finally exited the store with two shopping carts overflowing
with items, Marian could only sigh and roll her eyes. Sam
was excited about all of the items he bought on sale.

"Marian, Marian, get out of the car and come look at what I bought!" He insisted on opening each bag for her to inspect before he loaded everything in the trunk. Marian was aghast. He had purchased multiples of everything: shoes, slacks, and shirts in every color, along with numerous blouses for Marian. There were large quantities of household items, including twelve boxes of business envelopes and a carton of toilet tissue. Sam was animated and exuberant, and Marian was furious. Somehow she managed to keep her emotions in check.

"Sam, take some of these things back. We don't need all these envelopes and all of that toilet tissue. Keep the things you bought for yourself, but I don't need all of these blouses."

"What's wrong with you? Look at how much money I've saved! I'm not taking anything back," he yelled. With a slam of the trunk and an abrupt push of the shopping carts, Sam signaled that the discussion was over.

During their drive back to Chicago, Sam kept telling Marian how disrespectful she had been for asking him to return the items he had bought. Not wanting to start a big argument, Marian pretended to be asleep as Sam continued to rant.

She said a little prayer of thanks when they arrived home safely late that night. The Wal-Mart bags stayed exactly where Sam dropped them ... in the middle of the hall floor. Marian wasn't in any mood to deal with Sam's purchases. Tomorrow morning would be soon enough.

As Sam went into the den and turned on the TV, Marian got ready for bed. As exhausted as she was, though, she couldn't fall asleep. Her mind was filled with questions about

Sam's behavior. Finally, she got up and walked to the bookshelf. Taking two of Sam's psychology books, she settled on the couch to read.

When Marian finished looking at the books on manic-depression, she leaned back on the couch, making a mental checklist of all the symptoms Sam had been exhibiting. Marian was convinced she was finally beginning to have some answers about his erratic behavior. When Sam walked past the living room on his way upstairs, Marian called for him to join her. His eyes darted from Marian to the books that were lying on the table.

"You have no right looking through my books." Sam's voice was angry.

"You have no right to withhold information about your health," Marian shot back.

She had intended to have a calm talk with Sam, but their conversation quickly escalated into an ugly argument. Finally, she gave him an ultimatum. "I want you to call a doctor to set up an appointment for an evaluation. If you won't call, then I will. And if you refuse to see a doctor, then I will pack my things and leave."

Sam was stunned and Marian was determined.

—Chapter 5—

The Psychiatric Evaluation

"Are you ready, Sam?"

"Almost. I'm doing this for you, you know," Sam snapped. He grabbed his keys off the table and headed toward the car.

"It will help both of us," Marian replied as she climbed into the passenger seat.

She sat quietly as Sam maneuvered the car through the heavy morning traffic. Every traffic light turned from yellow to red, and Marian could feel Sam's anxiety building. To ease the tension, she tried to engage him in idle chatter, but was quickly silenced by a barrage of sarcastic complaints.

"You couldn't have scheduled this appointment at a worse time. Didn't you know the morning traffic would be horrendous? Shit, did you see what that jerk just did, cutting in front of us?"

As Sam gave two beeps to the horn and slammed on the brakes, Marian lurched forward. Knowing that the half-hour drive to the hospital would feel like an eternity, she let out a long sigh. There was nothing she could do to calm Sam down when he was in this kind of mood.

As they pulled into the hospital parking garage and found a parking space, Sam broke the silence. "Marian, don't leave me alone."

Marian thought of the confident, sociable man she had met at Sue's party. The changes she had seen in Sam were astounding.

"Don't worry, Sam. I'll be right here." She reached for his hand, which Sam kept jammed in his jacket pocket.

As Marian started walking toward the main entrance of the hospital, she realized that he was trailing behind. She slowed her pace in order to walk beside him. As they reached the elevator that would take them to the psychiatric floor, Marian turned to him. "Sam, are you all right?" His response was a cold stare back at her. In silence, they continued on to the third floor and found room 301.

While Sam checked in at the reception desk, Marian found two seats together in the waiting room. She took a magazine and started leafing through it. When Sam joined her, he was carrying a five-page questionnaire to fill out. He looked pale, tired, and irritable. Marian continued to flip through the magazine and tried to act nonchalant, as if sitting in a psychiatrist's office was an everyday occurrence for her. People came and went, asked questions, gave out personal information, and waited to be called for their appointments. Sam continued to answer the questions on the questionnaire, apparently remembering the dates of important milestones: births, deaths, marriages, and graduations. Just as Sam was finishing, a nurse came over and collected the written information. Then she asked them to follow her into another room, where Sam was told to remove his shirt. As the nurse left the room, she said that Dr. Shulman would be in momentarily.

"Do you want me to leave, Sam?" Marian asked

"No, you promised to stay with me."

Marian smiled as she reassured him. "That's fine, Sam. I won't leave. I just wanted to be sure."

Just then they heard a light tap on the door. A tall, scholarly-looking gentleman walked in. As the doctor entered the room, Marian caught a glimpse of Sam as he recoiled and shifted his weight on the examining table.

"Good morning, I am Dr. Shulman," he said with a smile. "You must be Sam, and you are Marian, I presume." He glanced from Sam to Marian and then back again to Sam.

Dr. Shulman flipped through the pages of Sam's questionnaire before moving to the examining table. He continued to talk as he checked Sam's eyes, nose, and throat.

"Quite a history you have here, Sam. You've been dealing with depression for some time, but I notice you aren't on any medication. Do you drink alcohol or take illegal drugs of any kind?"

"No," Sam answered.

"History of depression or other mood disorders in your family: father, mother, grandparents, siblings, or first cousins?"

"No."

Dr. Shulman continued talking while he examined Sam's neck and thyroid. "You mentioned here that your biological father died when you were a baby. What was the cause? Accident, illness, suicide?"

"I'm not sure. Suicide maybe."

"Any other history you remember?"

"No."

"Okay, Sam, you can get dressed now. When we're finished here, I want you to stop at the lab for blood work and a thyroid test." Dr. Shulman reached into a file cabinet and pulled out a depression scale. "Now I want you to fill this out the best you can, reflecting on the past year. Then get some lunch and let me see you back here at 2:00. We will talk more then."

Marian was overwhelmed at what she had just heard. Biological father ... suicide ... what are they talking about? Sam had never mentioned any of this to her. She was shocked, wondering how much more had been left unsaid. Not wanting to upset him more than he already was, she kept her questions to herself as she followed him to the lab.

After a lab worker took three vials of blood from Sam's left arm, they took the elevator back to the main floor and found the cafeteria.

Marian took a tray and started looking at the menu. "What do you want to eat?" She asked.

"I'm not hungry. Just get something for yourself."

After waiting in line for a bowl of soup, she walked to the table where Sam was drinking a cup of coffee.

"Are you sure you don't want something to eat?"

"No, I told you I'm not hungry." Sam looked sullen and dejected.

They sat quietly, both of them feeling the pain of uncertainty about what the end of the day would bring. Finally Sam broke the silence.

"It's 1:45. We should go back upstairs to the doctor's office. Or do you think we should just leave?"

Marian was startled by the question. "No, we are not going to leave without talking to the doctor. We've spent all this time here, so another hour won't matter." Her voice was louder than she meant it to be, and Sam gave her a disgusted look.

She felt irritated that he hadn't told her more about himself. She was also angry for allowing herself to be swept up in the excitement of a new relationship without asking more questions. Instead of following her heart, she knew she should have been more cautious, taking the time to get to know Sam better.

When they walked back into the reception area, the nurse immediately escorted them into a private office. While Sam read the certificates hanging on the wall, Marian took some educational pamphlets that were scattered on the coffee table. As they waited for the doctor to arrive, Sam became increasingly restless. Joining Marian on the sofa, he reached over and took her hand. He was trembling and his palm was sweaty. She gave his hand a reassuring squeeze as they waited for the doctor.

It wasn't long before the door opened. Dr. Shulman walked to the corner desk and sat down. While shuffling through the lab reports, he asked, "Did you have time to get some lunch?"

"Yes," Sam and Marian answered in unison.

"That's good. Well, your lab work came back fine. Nothing to worry about there. I would like to run the thyroid test again in six months."

Putting the papers down, he looked directly at Sam. "I've had a chance to look over the information you put on the questionnaire: the history of a very severe depression you experienced during your college years, the episode while you were in the Army that required your hospitalization, the mood-cycling from low to high. Although I would need to run more tests, I believe you have a classic case of manic-depression. Have you ever heard of that, Sam?"

"Yes."

"Do you understand the symptoms of that illness?"

"I think so."

"Marian, do you understand?"

"I ... I'm not sure."

Turning from Marian to Sam, the doctor replied, "This is not something you can 'wish away', Sam. Just in this past year, you have had three episodes of extreme lows and highs. By your own admission, it has created family and work problems. I'm recommending that you voluntarily go into the hospital. We can start you on some medication while we run additional tests. You will be monitored closely to determine the correct level of medication, and when we feel the dosage is correct and you're stable, you will be released. Sam, take a couple of days to think about this. Then let me know how you feel about hospitalization. Until then, here is a prescription for some medication that will help you."

Sam took the prescription from Dr. Shulman's outstretched hand and walked abruptly to the door. Turning to Marian, Dr. Shulman smiled. He shook Marian's hand and lingered for a moment.

"Good luck to both of you. And Marian, please seek help for yourself. This is going to be a rocky road for you also."

Somehow she managed to nod her head in agreement as she watched Dr. Shulman leave the room. Marian felt numb, questions swirling through her mind.

"Well, are you going to stand there gawking all day? I want to get the hell out of here." Sam's angry words broke the silence.

They hastily walked out of the hospital and found their car in the parking garage. Marian attempted to start a conversation, but Sam made it very clear he didn't want to talk about his so-called "illness" or the incompetent doctor who made the diagnosis.

By the time they arrived home, they were emotionally exhausted. Sam turned up the volume on the television and hid behind his newspaper. Marian took the pamphlets she had picked up at the doctor's office and went into the bedroom to read the information. When Sam came into the room to get ready for bed later that evening, he was visibly angry.

"What are you reading that shit for?" he snapped.

"I'm trying to figure out what is happening with you."

"So you believe what that asshole doctor said?"

"I believe he understands that your mood swings aren't normal."

"What do you know about being normal?"

"I just mean that you ..."

"Do you think you are normal?"

"Well ... what I meant to say ..."

"All that asshole doctor wants to do is to push pills on people."

"Sam, look ..."

"Why can't you just support me ... accept me the way I am? You just want to control me. You are just like my mother!"

Marian was stunned. "What does that mean?"

Without answering, Sam flopped onto the bed. Marian leaned over to put her arms around him, but he stayed on his side of the bed, stiff and unyielding. Marian rolled back to her side of the bed, wondering how to make things easier for him.

The next morning Marian awoke early and quietly headed to the kitchen. She sat at the table with her morning coffee, trying to focus on everything she had heard the previous day: manic-depression, father's suicide, hospitalization. The past 24 hours seemed like a bad dream.

She tried to comfort herself with something she had read in one of the pamphlets last night: manic-depression is manageable with appropriate medication. Although the whole situation seemed overwhelming, Marian finally convinced herself everything would be okay once Sam filled the prescription Dr. Shulman had given him.

When Sam entered the kitchen a few minutes later, Marian asked what he wanted for breakfast.

"I'm not hungry. I'll just have some coffee."

Marian tried to visit with him, but her attempt at small talk fell flat. Finally she gathered up enough courage to approach the subject of medication.

"I'm glad Dr. Shulman gave you a prescription. Do you want to get it filled on your way to work or do you want me to pick it up for you?"

Sam glared at her with an icy expression.

"I told you … I don't need any damn pills!"

He slammed the door on his way out of the house, and Marian was left alone to try and make sense of everything that was happening.

Days turned into weeks, and then into months. Sam concentrated on his job, trying to catch up on the work he had been neglecting. Marian, meanwhile, did her best to keep the household running smoothly. Although Sam refused to get the prescription filled, his mood did seem to level off. This seemed to be a sign to him that he didn't need the medication after all. But as Marian settled into her daily routine, she had serious doubts.

—Chapter 6—

CHRISTMAS IN IOWA

M ARIAN WAS SITTING AT HER EASEL ONE AFTERNOON, finishing up an oil painting she hoped to sell at an upcoming craft show. The sun streaming through the window made everything in the room sparkle with its reflection. She leaned back in her chair, basking in the sun's warmth. For the first time in months, she felt calm and relaxed.

Marian thought of last night's phone conversation with her kids. Charles and Edward had been filled with chatter about their favorite sports teams and were eager to tell her about the projects they planned to enter in the Science Fair at school. Susan had also been full of news about the upcoming weekend. She was going to the skating rink with a school group, followed by a sleep-over at her best friend's house.

Marian's trip back to Pennsylvania to see them had eased her mind. The decision to let them stay with their dad when she moved to Chicago seemed to be working out well. Although Marian often tried to find out how they felt about the changes in their lives, they usually brushed off her questions with the standard reply of, "Ah, everything is okay, Mom. Oh, and don't forget we're coming to see you soon."

"I can't wait!" she assured them. "We'll have lots of fun."

As Marian added a dab of green to her painting, she thought about her wonderful relationship with her kids, and wished Sam would make more of an effort with his own children. She felt sad whenever she thought of them.

Samantha was named after her father. Sam had described her as being bright and entertaining, doing almost anything to capture the attention of her dad. At the ripe old age of fourteen, she thought she knew almost everything there was to know, and, in order to get her opinions across, she loved to stubbornly argue with anyone near enough to listen. Sam said that, even though Samantha missed him a lot, she had a good life in Iowa with his first wife, Amy.

Sam had also told Marian how much Samantha adored George, her eleven-year-old half-brother from Sam's marriage to his second wife, Penny. George was an active child, and as long as there were games to play or a sister to tease, he was in his glory. He loved to be outdoors playing a game of flag football or shooting hoops with his friends.

From what Sam had told her, his divorce from Penny had been difficult for the children. The lives of George and Samantha had been turned upside down by the divorce and things would never again be the same for them. Although Marian thought it was very important for Sam to keep in close touch with his kids, at least for now she was content. She was sure everything would eventually work out.

Sam was continuing to feel well even though he still hadn't filled the prescription from Dr. Shulman. Marian put aside the nagging little thoughts she would occasionally have. After the first few turbulent months of their relationship, she knew it wasn't wise to rock the boat by asking Sam a lot of questions.

One thing Marian couldn't stop, though, was her desire for more information about the diagnosis Sam received from Dr Shulman. She didn't think she would ever forget what the doctor had said: "Sam, from the information you have given me regarding your life experiences, your relationship issues, and your mood swings, I am fairly certain that you have manic-depression."

Marian was still stunned whenever she replayed his words: "… you have manic-depression … manic-depression."

But what was even more confusing was the way Sam had responded to the doctor. Sam's face had shown no reaction to Dr. Shulman's words. It was as though he had heard those words before. Or was it just that he had needed time to get used to the diagnosis? Why hadn't he asked the doctor more questions, and why wasn't he willing to talk to Marian about how he was feeling? She wanted answers to these questions, but it wouldn't be now. This just wasn't the right time. Not now, when things were so calm in their household.

Sam's fun-loving personality had returned … the personality that had been so intriguing to her when they first met. As she continued working on her painting, she fondly remembered the day he had rushed through the front door after work, his hands behind his back and a wide grin on his face.

He had coyly said to her, "Marian, I have something for you. Do you want what is in my left hand or my right hand? Think long and hard before you answer!"

Marian had chosen his right hand, and with a flourish, he had handed her a beautiful bouquet of her favorite red and yellow flowers.

"What are these for?"

"I just wanted to buy flowers for my best gal," he had happily replied. "And Marian, will you marry me?"

Marian had been elated. "Oh, Sam. Yes, yes, yes, I'll marry you!" she had exclaimed as she threw her arms around his neck. This fun-loving, impulsive man was the Sam she had fallen in love with.

Marian gave a contented sigh as she remembered that special day. Turning back to her easel, she murmured to herself, "Hmm, I wonder which shade of blue I should use for the sky." She looked at the large selection of oils next to her before choosing a light azure color. She was hoping to finish the picture soon. She and Sam were busy making plans to go to Iowa for Christmas, and there was so much to do before the trip.

She was still painting when Sam came home from work. "Hi, hon," he said as he entered the room. "Wow, your picture looks great. Wish I could paint like that."

Marian beamed. Sam was becoming much more loving and attentive, and she was enjoying the peace that was settling over their lives.

"Oh, by the way, Sam, I received some college pamphlets in the mail today. I've always wanted to take the last few classes I need so I can get my degree. What do you think of that idea?"

"Sounds great! Maybe I'll even take a course or two at the same time." He stretched and relaxed on the couch as he continued. "Oh, I almost forgot to tell you. I've found a men's soccer team to join. I ate lunch with some guys at work and they told me about it."

Sam hadn't been talking much about his job, so Marian was glad to hear he had been socializing with his friends at work.

After dinner, they finished planning their trip to Iowa for the holidays. Marian was excited about finally getting to meet Sam's family. Christmas was her favorite time of year and she felt like a child waiting for Santa. She didn't think she could wait until the big day arrived!

The night before the trip, Sam and Marian loaded the car with their suitcases and found room in the back seat for all of the Christmas presents. Marian had painstakingly wrapped the gifts in colorful holiday paper, each one topped with a festive bow she had made herself.

The drive to Iowa the next morning was pleasant even though Marian had a bad case of the jitters. "What if Sam's kids don't like me?" she fretted. "And what about his parents? I know his mom wanted him to try to work things out with Penny."

As they entered Sam's hometown, Marian noticed the pretty tree-lined streets. Her anxiety increased as they pulled up to the house where Sam's parents lived. She immediately fell in love with the attractive two-story house. She liked the green shutters and admired the beautiful evergreen trees that bordered the yard. In her mind, she could almost imagine Sam as a young boy, swinging from the branches of the large shade tree or playing tag with his friends in the spacious front yard.

Before Sam even had a chance to shut off the car motor, Marian turned to him. Her face was lined with tension. "I'm afraid your family won't like me. What will happen then?"

Sam gave her hand a reassuring squeeze. "You're only the third woman I've brought home for them to meet!" he joked. "Of course they'll like you."

Marian gave a slight chuckle. "Sam, this isn't a good time to tell your family about our plans to get married. Everyone, especially your kids, need some time to get to know me.

Promise me that you won't say anything."

Sam gave her a wink. "Don't worry, Marian. Everything will work out just fine."

Out of the corner of her eye, she saw the front door open.

"Only the third woman, only the third woman," played in her head as Sam's relatives swarmed around the car, eager to give him a hug and to meet the new woman in his life.

He proudly introduced Marian to everyone: his kids, parents, grandparents, and siblings. Samantha and George immediately began talking over each other with spirited enthusiasm. "Hey, Dad ... guess what, Dad ... wait 'til you see what I have ... did you bring me some presents, Dad?"

Sam's parents were pleasant and warm. "If my son brought another woman home under these circumstances, I'm pretty sure I wouldn't be this gracious," Marian thought to herself. She noticed how much Sam resembled his mother: the sparkling blue eyes, the soft-spoken voice, and the charm they both displayed. His dad was distinguished-looking, a tall man with a kind-looking face and a deep voice that was authoritative and confident.

As soon as Sam finished introducing her to everyone, Marian began to relax.

"See, this isn't so bad," he whispered as they walked into the house. A huge Christmas tree filled one corner of the living room. It was decorated with an odd assortment of ornaments, and Marian could tell each one had a personal meaning for the family. Multi-colored lights and strands of garlands completed the tree, and she thought it was the most beautiful one she had ever seen.

She noticed delicious smells coming from the kitchen

and remembered that she had been too nervous to eat break-fast that morning.

"Please make yourself at home, Marian. We're getting ready to take the ham out of the oven, so we'll be eating soon," said Sam's dad.

"Is there anything I can do to help?" Marian asked.

"Nothing right now." Sam's mom put some steaming vegetables into a bowl. "We'll let you do all the dishes after we eat!" she joked.

Everyone found a place to sit around the large table in the dining room. Marian looked at the huge assortment of food before them: meat, mashed and sweet potatoes, Sam's favorite kind of dressing, two bowls of vegetables, and homemade bread that Sam's grandma had made. As Marian took a slice of the bread, she recalled the stories Sam had told her about his grandparents: helping his grandpa with projects in the garage and stopping at their house after school to grab some warm cookies his grandma had just taken out of the oven.

As everyone started eating, she looked at the warm friendly faces surrounding her. Yes, being with Sam's family for Christmas was everything she had hoped for. This was turning out to be a special holiday.

Once the huge meal was over and the clean-up was finished, everyone gathered in the living room. Under the Christmas tree was a vast array of packages, each one a different shape and size.

"George, do you want to be 'Santa' and pass out the gifts?" Sam asked.

"Wow, yeah!" he exclaimed, jumping to his feet.

As the gifts were passed out, Marian noticed that the

recipients took time to shake, squeeze, and thoroughly examine each package, trying to guess what the decorated box contained. She was a bit melancholy that she wasn't spending Christmas with her own children. And yet, she felt a great deal of pleasure in being a part of this family. She loved Sam, and even though their first few months together had been challenging, she knew this was where she belonged.

Sam had talked about his family and what his life was like as he grew up in this idyllic little town. Now she was seeing for herself all the people and places he had talked about so fondly. He loved and respected his parents and knew that they deeply loved him as well. He and his three siblings had grown up in a warm caring environment, and as Marian watched his family interacting, she knew Sam had had a wonderful childhood in this place ... and with these people.

As soon as the last of the gifts had been opened and all of the wrapping paper and bows had been thrown away, Samantha spied a large stack of board games.

"Hey, Dad. How about playing a game?" she asked eagerly.

"I wanna' play too," shouted George. "And I bet I'll win!"

Marian watched intently as Sam and the kids engaged in a 'winner-take-all' game. They chattered happily as they moved their game pieces around the board, and the kids were delighted whenever Sam made a wrong move.

The rest of the day passed quickly. As Marian settled into bed that night, she snuggled next to Sam and sighed.

"This has been a great holiday. Your kids are wonderful and the rest of your family ... well, I love them all."

The next morning, Sam's mother prepared a large breakfast for everyone before Sam and Marian gathered their belongings for the trip back to Chicago. Once they had packed the car, Sam's father was the first to speak.

"Marian, we have enjoyed meeting you. Please come again soon."

Sam had an impish grin on his face as he turned toward his family. "You'll be seeing a lot of Marian from now on. We're going to get married!"

Samantha and George stood quietly beside their dad, looking stunned by this piece of news. Marian glanced at the rest of the family and saw the looks of astonishment on their faces. Finally, Sam's mom spoke.

"Uh, congratulations, Sam and Marian. This is quite a surprise. When ... uh ... I don't really know what to say. Have you chosen a date for the wedding?"

"As far as I'm concerned, the sooner the better," Sam cheerfully answered. "Hey, kids, what do you think of our news?"

George started scuffing his shoes in the gravel driveway, avoiding his father's gaze. Samantha walked up to her grandpa and leaned against him. "I guess it's okay," she mumbled.

"Well, we'll be in touch as soon as we finalize our plans." Sam turned toward his kids and gave each of them a big hug. "Be good and I'll see you again soon." Samantha had tears in her eyes and George's lower lip trembled a bit. Saying good-bye to their dad was such a difficult thing.

After Sam's unexpected announcement, Marian found it difficult to face his family. She was embarrassed by the way Sam had blurted out the news. She also felt a profound sadness for his kids. Somehow she managed to whisper a quiet "Thanks so much for a wonderful holiday," before she escaped into the front seat of the car.

Marian was fuming as Sam pulled out of the driveway. "Sam, how could you have been so insensitive? That was a horrible way to tell your kids about our plans. They barely know me…and all of a sudden, you're telling them that we're going to get married! I thought we had agreed this wasn't a good time to tell them." Her fists were clenched as angry tears rolled down her cheeks.

Sam calmly turned to Marian. "Well, they had to be told sometime, and I figured the sooner the better. Don't worry. They'll adjust okay to the news. Hey, before we leave town, let me show you some of the sights. I bet you've never seen a tiny place like this before."

"Sam … I'm furious that you ignored my feelings. I'm in no mood to take a tour."

Sam acted as though he didn't hear her. He turned the corner and started driving down Main Street. He pointed to the tiny café where he and his buddies had often gone after school for a bag of chips and a cold bottle of Coke. "Sometimes we'd eat Sunday dinner there too," Sam explained. "They had the best meatloaf … except for Mom's, that is. Oh, yeah, I almost forgot. I loved their pumpkin pie."

Beside the café was the local grocery store. Hanging from a rusty-looking chain was a sign "Martin's Grocery Store" and just outside the door was a wooden bench. Sam told her the retired gents always sat there to watch the activity along the street while they talked about the latest town gossip.

Marian had never seen a town this small, and she found herself getting caught up in Sam's stories as they drove past the rest of the downtown businesses. Then Sam pulled onto one of the side streets. Marian noticed older homes mixed in with newer ones, impressed by their neat tidy appearances. At the end of the street was a huge brick building. Sam stopped in front of it and proudly said, "This is where I went to school. See that empty lot behind the school? That's where my friends and I played, especially in the summertime. We'd ride our bikes over here and spend the whole afternoon goofing around. We wouldn't go back home until it was almost dark."

"But was it safe for you to be out on the streets without a grown-up nearby? Didn't your mom and dad worry about you?"

Sam smiled. "Marian, this has always been a perfect place for a kid to grow up. People always look out for one another in a town like this. There may be a lot of gossiping that goes on, and you always have your busy-bodies who want to know everything about everybody. But they're good people and they always take care of each other. I was a lucky kid."

As they drove out of town, Marian's anger toward Sam began to subside. Maybe he was right. His family needed to know that she was going to be a permanent part of his life. She sat back, reflecting on everything she had seen and heard during this Christmas holiday. After meeting Sam's family and seeing where he had grown up, she felt closer than ever to him.

—Chapter 7—

The First Wife

Marian was looking forward to getting a little rest during the drive back to Chicago. It had been a hectic Christmas and she was tired.

They had just left Sam's peaceful hometown when he turned to her and asked, "See the farmland on either side of this road?"

"Yes, it goes on for miles," Marian said as she looked out the car window. "Someone could get lost around here for days."

"Well, someone did disappear once."

Marian was intrigued, listening quietly as Sam continued.

"Are you sure you're ready to hear about some of your husband's adventures?" he asked.

"Sure, although by now, don't I know almost everything about you?"

"Hardly! Let me fill you in on a little more about my first marriage. Where should I start? Well, after I got out of the Army, Amy and I came back here to live. We had some pretty rough times. One evening, we got into an argument. It wasn't a bad one, but I decided to leave for a while to cool off. When I went to get the car keys, she wouldn't let me have them. I tried to wrestle them out of her hand, but I accidentally twisted her arm and she got really mad. She said she was going to call the sheriff and have me arrested for abuse. So as soon as she started to call the cops, I ran outside and hid in the corn field behind our house. It wasn't long before I started getting cold and tired, so I tried going back into the house, but she wouldn't let me in. I could see her through the kitchen window, but she just ignored me. So I kicked the door in. After all, it was my house, too, and she had no right to keep me out. Just then, I heard the sheriff's car pull into the driveway, so I knew I had to get out of there or I'd be arrested. I spent the next few hours hiding in the cornfield again. Every once in a while, I heard a police helicopter overhead and saw its spotlight. I was determined that no one would find me."

Marian sat in stunned silence as she listened to Sam. "Then what happened?" she asked.

There was no way I was going to stay around Amy, so I hid in the fields at night. Then during the day, I broke into empty houses so I could get some food, a change of clothes, and a little cash. Eventually I managed to get to Chicago and then on to Seattle."

Marian sat with her hands folded, staring out the window as they drove by acres and acres of farmland. Occasionally she saw farmhouses in the distance. As she listened to Sam's story, she felt an overwhelming sense of sadness. She wiped tears from her eyes, and then reached over and took Sam's hand.

"Sam, why didn't you just stay and work things out with Amy?"

"Oh, she would have had me arrested. You don't know how vindictive Amy could be."

"Seeing you so angry probably scared her."

Sam's mood changed abruptly and he jerked his hand

from Marian's grasp.

"There you go again, Marian, taking everybody else's side instead of supporting me."

"No, Sam, I'm not taking sides. I'm just trying to understand how Amy may have felt. What a sad situation for all of you."

"That's not even half of it," Sam announced.

"Well, tell me more. What did you do when you got to Seattle?"

"Oh, not much. I'll tell you more later." Sam sounded irritable.

Marian could tell he had shut down emotionally, and at least for now, their conversation was over. She occasionally tried to talk to Sam about the college classes she was planning to take or about his upcoming soccer games, but Sam didn't talk during the rest of the trip home. The only sound came from the radio. He turned the dial to a sports station, where an annoying call-in guest was riled up about some asinine player who fumbled the ball. Sam appeared to listen intently while he ignored Marian.

Her heart was breaking as she thought of Sam's story. Since she had seen flashes of his anger during their time together, she knew how volatile he could be. But why had Amy been so quick to call the sheriff? Marian remembered Sam's appointment with Dr. Shulman. Could this situation with Amy have been the result of a manic episode? She had lots of questions, but Sam didn't seem to be willing to provide the answers ... at least not today.

As farmland continued to flash by, the only thing Marian could think of was Sam, running and running and running. Never looking back. All alone, without any belongings, and too scared to reach out to anyone for help.

—Chapter 8—

THE LETTER

T HE HOLIDAYS WERE OVER AND THE NEW YEAR ARRIVED
without much fanfare. Nothing could erase Marian's
memories of the wonderful Christmas she and Sam had
spent with his family. She would often smile as she remembered something that had happened during their visit to
Iowa.

Marian sat at the kitchen table, her date book and the
calendar spread in front of her. She would be starting her
college classes soon, and she could barely contain her excitement about going back to school. She wanted her college
degree and was determined that, finally, she would be able
to achieve her goal. So many other things had always taken
precedence over her class work, but this time nothing was
going to stop her.

"Sam, when you said good-bye to Samantha and George,
you told them they could come to Chicago for a visit. Should
we plan that trip before I get busy with my classes?"

"I've had enough celebrating with my family to last a
life-time. In fact, I would have been happier staying home
over the holidays; just the two of us. Now I suppose you'll
start in on me: "What is wrong with you? Don't you care
about anyone besides yourself?" You can be so condescend-
ing sometimes and you always want to have the last word
on every subject. I just don't have the energy to argue with
you right now."

Marian stared at Sam, not knowing what to say. Finally she managed a quiet "Ok, let's skip their visit for now. After all, we were just together for Christmas."

"And besides," Sam continued, "I really need to start spending more time in the office. I have to write several reports and get caught up on some projects."

"That's fine, Sam, but please, at least call and let the kids know we'll be busy for a few weeks."

"There you go again, always trying to control everything. Just like when you decided I needed to see that damn doctor. I knew he'd try to push medicine on me. I'm not going down that road again. Don't you understand? Sometimes I just want to be left alone. Surely that isn't too much to expect."

Marian watched as Sam stomped out of the kitchen and into the den.

"What on earth ..." she thought. "Why is he saying these things?" From where she was sitting, she could see him as he sat down at his desk and pulled out a legal pad. She knew it was best to leave him alone when he was in this kind of mood.

A couple of hours later, Sam walked into the kitchen and handed her a letter. "Here, read this. Maybe it'll explain some things," he said as he left the room.

Dear Marian,

Our relationship seems to be off-track lately. Your attention is more on the kids and going back to school instead of on me. You always have so many questions, and you never seem satisfied with the answers I give. Can't you just relax and leave the past alone? It's hard enough for me to think about the present, let alone what has happened in the past.

Yes, because of your snooping, you've figured out that I have depression problems and probably some mania too. My first depression was when I went away to college. I never mentioned it to anybody, but going from a quiet life in a small town to living on a big college campus was lonely and frightening. During that depression, my world slowed down to a crawl, the everyday chatter of the people around me was irritating, and the littlest sounds were magnified. I felt like everyone was yelling.

Even a nice sunny day seemed dull. I felt tired, like I had heavy chains wrapped around my legs. I lost all my confidence and felt numb and detached from the world around me.

But then the depression went away just as suddenly as it had come. The rest of my college days went fast. If I was depressed during that time, I didn't notice it. I joined ROTC, and in my junior year, I met the girl of my dreams. I thought my high moods were because of my new relationship with Amy.

After college, Amy and I got married, and I did my tour of duty with the Army. Marian, it's hard for me to talk about those days with Amy because we had so many good times together. We traveled, met lots of interesting people, and of course the best part was when Samantha was born. So when you ask me questions about my life with Amy, it's upsetting for me.

If Amy and I hadn't gone back to Iowa to live after I got out of the Army, things between us would have been different. Anyway, Amy and my mother ultimately betrayed me and stuck me in a mental hospital. I was smarter than any of the doctors and nurses, though, and I managed to escape from there. That's when I went to Seattle. I met Penny during that very dark time in my life. She didn't seem to care that I had walked away from a mental hospital and was living under an assumed name. I was very spiritual during that time, and Penny shared those experiences with me. She supported my decisions and was even willing to move away from her family so I could live closer to Samantha. She very seldom challenged what I said or what I wanted to do.

Penny and I were so happy when George was born. In fact, things were great until I started coming out of one of my depressions. We started fighting about stupid things: money, bills, how to discipline George. We were definitely pulling away from each other.

It was during that rough time in my marriage that I met you...my soul-mate. And now you are disappointing me with your talk about medicine and mental evaluations. It's not so bad when I'm depressed because you don't have to deal with me, and you can do what you want to do. And when I'm high, you like the special gifts I buy you and it doesn't matter how much money we spend. Life really isn't so bad, is it?

But if you still want me to, I'll check in with Dr. Shulman again. I'll even fill the prescription he gave me. I'll do it just for you.

I love you. Your Sam

—Chapter 9—

AND LIFE GOES ON

FOR THE NEXT FEW YEARS, LIFE APPEARED TO SETTLE INTO
somewhat of a normal routine. Happy occasions such as
births, graduations, and weddings blended in with illnesses
and deaths—all a part of life's journey. However, Marian's
and Sam's life had an additional component to it. Their time
together was measured by episodes of mania and depression: lost jobs, going into debt, infidelity, and hospitalization, followed by a peaceful calm until the cycle repeated
itself. Sam would faithfully take his medication for months
at a time, but then would unexpectedly decide he no longer
needed it.

As Marian learned about the medical history of Sam's
family, she discovered that there had been cases of depression on both his mother's and father's side of the family.
Two uncles had died in mental hospitals, three cousins had
been diagnosed with manic-depression, and as Samantha
and George grew into young adulthood, they had begun to
exhibit symptoms of the illness also.

As the years passed, Marian settled into a caregiver's role
with Sam. It wasn't planned that way ... it just seemed to
happen naturally. She would ocasionally count the pills in
Sam's medicine bottle, reminding him that he needed to stay
on his medication. She did her best to keep the home environment as stress-free as possible, and scheduled appointments every 3 months for Sam's blood work. When friends

invited them to social events, she made excuses about why they wouldn't be able to attend, and she cancelled visits with the kids whenever Sam was depressed. As a teenager, she had assumed the responsibility of caring for her younger siblings, trying to make things better for them. Now she found herself repeating that role as she tried to make things better for Sam.

Couples' counseling soon turned into individual sessions for Marion. Even though she was disappointed when Sam would no longer go with her, she looked forward to her own weekly sessions with the counselor. She began to gain insight into why she had left her family and friends to be with Sam.

When the counselor asked why she was staying with him, Marian gave the usual reasons: "I love him ... I can't go through another emotional divorce...I worry about what a divorce would do to the kids ..." Although the reasons for some of her decisions began to make sense to her, she was still unable to completely answer that one question.

As difficult as it was for her to deal with her own issues, Marian was saddest as she saw Sam's kids struggling to understand their father. When they were younger, it had been easier to cover up Sam's anger and to deal with the emotional wall he built around himself. She would tell them: "Your dad's in bed because he's tired ... He didn't really mean to yell at you...He's not upset with you, he's upset about something else." Marian would often tell Sam, "The kids need you, and they love you so much." Sam would respond by saying, "What good is that if I can't feel their love?"

Sam was either the "good dad" when he was in a manic high, or he was the "bad dad" during the times he was angry and depressed. For his children, never knowing which "dad" they would encounter was something that continued to confuse them.

The Roller Coaster Ride

—Chapter 10—

THE RETURN TO '89

MARIAN'S FLASHBACK OF THE PAST 18 YEARS LEFT HER feeling exhausted. She had no sense of time as she began to stir, knowing she had to face the day. She wondered if the yard sale was over.

"I can't spend any more time thinking about the past," she said to herself. She got out of bed and headed toward the stairs. As she turned the corner, there was Sam, coming up the stairs toward her, taking 2 steps at a time. She quickly stepped to the side to avoid a head-on collision. As Sam got closer, she saw his dilated glassy eyes and the purplish bulging veins in his neck.

He was in a rage. "I want you out of here! Out of here, do you hear me? Out of here before I come back!"

Sam turned around and jumped to the bottom of the stairs, yelling at her as he rushed out the front door: "I have business to take care of. There are notes for you on the table. Do what I say. There will be consequences if you disobey me."

Marian stood still until she heard Sam's car pull out of the driveway. Trembling, she took a deep breath to calm down. Questions swarmed through her mind. Where's he going? What's this all about? What business could he possibly have on a Saturday morning?

She went into the dining room and found the notes he had left. This had become Sam's usual way of communicating with her when his moods were cycling. Her hands shook as she shoved the notes into her pocket.

Knowing she needed some advice about how to handle this latest crisis, she picked up the phone.

"Dr. Shuman's office … please hold," the familiar voice said. Since it was Saturday, Marian was relieved that someone was in the office.

Marian waited impatiently until Dr. Shuman's nurse finally came on the line. Marian told her about Sam's condition and asked to speak directly to the doctor. Almost immediately she heard Dr. Shuman's voice. Marian recapped the events of the last 24 hours.

"Marian, has he threatened you or been physically aggressive toward you?" the doctor asked.

"Well, so far he has just been verbally aggressive," Marian answered.

"Do you think he will harm himself?"

"I don't know. He hasn't tried to harm himself before … at least not that I know of."

The doctor paused before going on. "Try and get him to go to the emergency room. The best outcome will be if he checks himself into the hospital. If he refuses to go … and that is likely because of the state he's in … then you must leave the house. Do not stay there. Without any medical intervention, his mood will continue to escalate. Let me know what happens."

Marian continued to cradle the phone in her hand as she leaned against the desk. The sun was shining through the window of the small study and she watched as tiny dust specks danced in the sun's reflection. The seriousness of what was happening was a sharp contrast to the beautiful weather outdoors. She glanced at the mantle clock and realized it wasn't even noon yet. So much had happened in such a short period of time.

Still feeling shaky and unsure of what to do next, Marian started toward the kitchen to fix a cup of tea. As she walked through the house, she was struck by how orderly each room appeared to be. Upon closer inspection, she realized that many items had been removed: a chair from the study, a lamp and table from the living room, and dishes from the china cabinet in the dining room. Marian was surprised to discover that even canned and packaged food had been removed from the pantry. What had Sam done with everything? Had he sold these things, thrown them away, what?? What on earth was he thinking?

Marian sat down at the kitchen table, trying to absorb everything that was happening. Then she remembered the notes Sam had left for her. She took the scraps of paper out of her pocket and laid them carefully on the table. Written in large handwriting were some rambling instructions:

"This house is no longer yours. Remove your things immediately. I can not be held responsible for what I might do with them."

"If you stay, you will be responsible for half of the expenses."

"You used 4 stamps that I paid for. Reimburse me immediately."

"You are free to live your own life."

"I paid for the groceries. You are not to eat anything out of the refrigerator."

"When you leave, return all of the keys to me immediately. Be gone before I get back."

"I divided the refrigerator space down the middle.
Don't let your food touch my food."

Realizing that Sam could come back at any time, Marian picked up the notes and ran upstairs. She took 2 suitcases from the hall closet … one for Sam and one for herself..and dropped them onto the bed. Moving quickly, she began filling them with clothing.

Marian's plan was to give Sam an ultimatum: "Either you go to the hospital, Sam, or I will leave you." She had used this plan once before when he needed to check into the hospital. But would it work again this time?

Just as she finished packing and was lugging the suitcases down the stairs, she heard the phone ring. By the time she managed to say hello, there was a click as the caller hung up.

"Sam, was that you?" she yelled into the phone.

Marian knew she had a lot to do before Sam came home. She rummaged through the desk drawer and file cabinet, locating important papers and documents she might need. Grabbing a few personal items, she stuffed everything into a large cardboard box. She managed to drag the box into the pantry and slipped it into the back of a large cupboard for safe-keeping.

Perspiration beaded on her forehead and her body ached from tension. She hoped that a breath of fresh air would help calm her. As she walked outdoors, she saw that everything had been cleaned up from the early-morning sale. When she walked to the garage and opened the door, she saw boxes stacked from the floor to the ceiling. Looking inside some of the boxes, she saw left-over items from the sale. Thrown in with those items were clothing and bags filled with papers. A wave of rage engulfed Marian.

Gasping for breath, she screamed, "WHY, WHY!"

The emotion and turmoil of the day had drained Marian of all energy. She went indoors and collapsed on the couch, soon falling into a fitful sleep. The next thing she knew, she was awakened by the ringing of the phone. By now the room was dark and she had no idea what time it was. Marian fumbled to reach the phone.

"Hello."

A woman's voice asked to speak to Sam.

"Who is calling?" Marian inquired.

"This is Barbara. Is Sam there?"

"Maybe I can help you." Marian took a deep breath.

"I'm answering Sam's personal ad, the one for a soulmate. Who are you?"

"I am Sam's wife," she managed to spit out.

"What??" Then the line went dead.

Throughout the rest of the evening, the phone continued to ring, but Marian refused to answer it. She felt humiliated and enraged at the thought that Sam was advertising for another woman. How dare he ... Finally, since there was still no sign of Sam, she turned the deadbolt lock on the door so he couldn't get in. Then she slumped on the couch, hoping that sleep would come quickly to block out the awful memories of that day.

Early the next morning, Marian was jolted awake by loud knocking. There was Sam, balancing three sacks of groceries as he tried to open the door. Marian hesitated for a moment, then unlocked the dead-bolt. Sam quickly pushed his way in the door and headed toward the kitchen. He was in an exuberant mood, talking nonstop as he unloaded the groceries. Just then, he saw the suitcases Marian had packed the night before. Suddenly his mood changed and he began to frantically question her.

"Where are you going?" Sam demanded to know.

"It's not where I am going, Sam. It's where you are going."

"Don't play coy with me, Marian. Tell me right now what's going on."

Marian took a deep breath. Her heart was beating so fast she was sure he could hear it pounding. "Sam, I called Dr. Shuman yesterday, and he wants you to check into the hospital for an evaluation."

Sam glared at Marian and started to move toward her. She quickly took a step back as she continued. "We've been through this before, Sam. You haven't been on your medication for over a month and you're quickly going into a manic high. Do you remember what happened the last time you stopped taking your meds? Well, do you?"

Marian's voice continued to get louder and louder. "Sam, if you don't start taking your medicine, you will lose everything: this house, your job, our marriage. How many times can we start over??" Tears stung her cheeks.

As she reached her arms toward Sam, he jumped back as though a bolt of lightning had struck him, then just as quickly moved toward her. Before Marian could even react, Sam had swiftly put his hands on her shoulders. His face was bright red, his eyes sunken and twitching.

Marian's fury suddenly turned to fright as Sam began to scream. "Your face is turning green ... your head is spinning. You are the devil!! You are the devil!!"

He began pushing her toward the door. "Get out, get out before I ... "

As Marian ran toward the garage, she heard the front door slam behind her. She quickly grabbed the extra set of car keys she had hidden earlier, and drove away without looking back. She took the shortest route to her best friend's house and hysterically told Liz what had just happened with Sam.

"Marian, you're safe here and you can stay with me as long as you want to. But you can't go on like this any longer. You've spent all these years trying to help Sam. Now you have to protect yourself. And you also need to get some advice about how to deal with Sam's psychotic behavior." Marian nodded in agreement as she erupted into uncontrollable sobbing.

She waited a couple of days before picking up the phone. As difficult as it would be, she had to call his kids to let them know what was happening. She asked if they had heard from their dad. "Not a word," they told her.

By the end of the week, Marian couldn't wait any longer. She had to know how Sam was doing. She jumped in the car and drove by their house. Sam's car was gone, so she parked a few houses down the street and cautiously walked up to the front door. Three morning newspapers were still on the front porch, and she saw no signs of activity.

Just to be on the safe side, Marian rang the door bell and waited for a few seconds. Then, with a feeling of dread, she slipped her key into the lock. As the door swung open, she stuck her head in and yelled Sam's name.

"Sam, it's me, Marian. Are you here, Sam?"

The house was eerily silent. Marian couldn't believe what

she saw as she slowly walked from room to room. All of the pictures had been taken off the walls, every piece of furniture had been removed, and even the bed linens and towels were gone. Every sign of Marian's existence had been eliminated: the house was barren. There was nothing left to bear witness to her life with Sam. Not a picture. Not a hair brush. Nothing.

—Chapter 11—

THE SEARCH WARRANT

MARIAN COLLAPSED ONTO THE FLOOR, UNABLE TO comprehend how her life with Sam had disintegrated into nothingness. The emotions of betrayal, sorrow, and anger collided within her.

"How could you do this to me, Sam?" she moaned. She continued to sit on the floor, shocked by the sight of the empty house.

The ringing phone startled her back to reality.

"Hello," she said in a dazed voice.

"Hello, with whom am I speaking?" the male voice asked.

"This is Marian Duncan."

"Marian, this is Captain Davis from the Highland Police Department. Are you related to Sam Duncan?"

"Yes, he is my husband."

Captain Davis continued. "We have a warrant to search your house, so a patrol cruiser will be arriving shortly."

Marian could barely get the words out. "Yes, ok, I'll be here." The palms of her hands were damp with perspiration and her throat felt tight. Marian took a deep breath, struggling to control herself.

By the time Marian hung up the phone, two armed police officers were walking up the sidewalk. She was shaking as they flashed their badges and introduced themselves. They showed her the search warrant and explained that they would need to look through the entire house, including the attic and basement.

"I don't understand ... what is this all about?" she asked the officers.

"We'll explain everything as soon as we're finished."

As they headed up the stairs, Marian walked outside and sat down on the front stoop. She couldn't stand the thought of being in the house. Even though there were no belongings left, Marian felt violated at the thought of her house being searched.

Her head was pounding and she was terrified. After all, she was in the presence of two armed policemen, and more importantly, she had no idea where Sam was or if he might suddenly show up. She listened as the officers opened closet doors and searched through kitchen cupboards.

After the officers inspected the inside of the house, they headed outdoors to continue their search.

Marian turned toward them. Her face was a chalky white and she had trouble catching her breath. "Excuse me. Would it be okay if I call a friend to come and be with me?"

The taller officer looked at her kindly. "I think that's a good idea, Mrs. Duncan."

As the officers searched the garage, Marian sat on the stoop in utter disbelief at what was happening. She was relieved when Liz's car finally pulled up to the curb.

"Marian, what's going on?? Do you know what this is all about?" Marian could only shake her head in response to Liz's questions.

It didn't take long for the officers to finish looking through the garage.

"Mrs. Duncan, may we ask you a few questions?" Marian

nodded.

"Did Sam stay here at the house last night? Where did you stay last night? When did you last have contact with Sam? Where can we reach you if we have any more questions?"

Marian finally gathered the courage to ask some questions of her own. "What is this all about? Why do you have a search warrant? Is Sam in some kind of trouble?"

They explained that Sam had been arrested that morning and was being held at the county jail. Tears stung her eyes as she tried to comprehend what they were telling her.

As Marian watched the squad car drive away, she turned to Liz. "I need to go to the jail right now so I can see Sam. I have to find out what's going on."

"I'll drive you to the jail if you insist on going, but I really think you need to take some time before making that decision."

Marian knew her friend was right. She expected to get a call from Sam right away, asking for bail money or wanting to know when she was coming to see him. No call came. A week passed before she finally decided to go to the jail. When Sam refused to see her, she was stunned.

Marian wasted no time as she headed toward the bailiff's office. "My husband was arrested several days ago and he has refused to see me. Please ... tell me what the charges are.

The bailiff patiently explained the situation to Marian. A hearing would be held soon and the charges against Sam were serious: resisting arrest, destruction of property, and burglary. As Marian left the jail, she was stunned by all the trouble he was in.

A few days later, Sam called. "Hey, Marian. I really need

to see you."

"You're in a lot of trouble, Sam. When you wouldn't see me, I talked to the bailiff. I just don't understand how you could ..." Marian stopped in midsentence. "I'll be there to see you this afternoon."

Since Sam's hearing was coming up soon, there was a lot for them to talk over. Marian wanted to know more about the charges, and she needed to hire a good lawyer to defend him.

When Marian arrived at the jail that afternoon, she showed some identification and was admitted to the waiting area by a security officer. She was surprised by how much she wanted to see Sam. Her anger toward him had begun to subside, and she wanted to make sure he was okay.

Marian sat down along with all the other visitors, watching as prisoners were led into the room one by one. She did a double-take as she saw Sam heading toward her. He walked slowly, his shoulders hunched, his hair looking grayer.

As he sat down across from her, he looked dazed and confused. Instead of looking into Sam's crystal-clear, aquamarine eyes, Marian was now peering into the dark, murky eyes of mental illness. Sam immediately started nitpicking.

"Why has it taken you so damn long to visit me? You have no idea how disgusting this place is, and the food is terrible. Didn't you even comb your hair before you came? It looks awful."

Marian was astounded. She sat and looked at Sam. Was that all he could focus on ... her hair ... while their world was going up in flames?

—Chapter 12—

Now What Do I Do?

TIME WAS A BLUR AS MARIAN TRIED TO HELP SAM. She hired the best attorney she could find to represent him. When Sam fired him, she had been furious.

"I don't need any damn lawyer. I know as much as he does, and besides ... all lawyers are crooks. I'll just defend myself," Sam had stated angrily.

Marian watched his moods cycle from high to low as he languished in jail for another month. He went from being verbose, exuberant, and frenetic to being depressed, discouraged, and aloof. By now, she was all too familiar with his mood swings. Marian was frustrated and sad, knowing it was impossible for Sam to be on any medication as long as he was in jail.

One evening, Marian invited Liz to their favorite restaurant for dinner. "This is my way of saying 'thank you' for all of your support," Marian explained. "I don't know what I would have done without your help these past few weeks."

"Glad to help out. After all, we're best friends. By the way, how are the kids handling all of this?"

"It has been really hard on his kids ... and on mine too. They have been taking turns coming back to Chicago to see Sam and to help me with all of the legal and personal things I have to handle."

Marian reflected on the visits that she and the kids had made to the jail.

"Sam is usually so angry whenever we go to see him. And he has been trying to turn us against each other. He writes these long letters to us, full of accusations and demands. And Liz, he even threatens us with physical violence sometimes. We're afraid of what he might do."

Liz encouraged Marian to continue.

"The kids have done their best to support him, and they've tried to ignore his hateful letters. But I think they've finally had all they can take. They just want to distance themselves from this whole mess."

Liz took a sip of wine. "And what about you, Marian?"

"I'm ... I guess I'm holding up pretty well. I'm trying not to make any major decisions while things are so chaotic. It's really sad to see Sam destroying all the important relationships in his life."

It wasn't long after her dinner with Liz that Marian was notified about the date of Sam's hearing. She slowly walked into the courthouse, sad at the thought of what was ahead for him. The lawyers had done some plea-bargaining, so the hearing didn't last long. Sam pleaded guilty to the charges in exchange for a shorter sentence and was transferred to a dingy cell in the State Prison.

Marian gave him a few days to adjust to his new surroundings before she made the trip to see him. A light rain began to fall as she pulled onto the prison grounds. Marian's mood matched the desolate weather as she studied the dismal surroundings. There was a small outdoor exercise area encircled with barbed wire. She thought of how much Sam loved to be outdoors ... about his excitement whenever he played soccer or joined in a pick-up basketball game.

Marian slowly entered the visitors' area of the prison.

The walls were a non-descript tan color, and she noticed the worn tiles on the floor. Along each wall were shabby-looking chairs and sofas. As she waited for what seemed like hours, she studied the faces of the other visitors, wondering about their life stories and what brought them to this place.

Finally, a female guard patted her down and led her to another smaller room. Everywhere she looked in the hot crowded room, armed guards were watching every move she made. As she sat down on a long wooden bench, she was miserable. "Sam and I should be home enjoying a quiet evening together or vacationing by the ocean," she mumbled. Images of a peaceful life with Sam flashed through her mind.

She was taken aback when she saw Sam file into the room. He seemed more alert than the last time she had seen him, and his expression was softer than usual. When he spotted Marian, his face lit up. He smiled as he joined her on the bench.

"Marian, guess what?"

"What, Sam?"

"I saw the doctor yesterday, and he said I need to take Lithium. He also recommended something else ... depa-something-or-other."

Marian was stunned. It was as though this was the first time anyone had ever told him he needed medication. Why had they been struggling over this issue for all of these years??

Marian's voice was flat. "Why do you need medicine now?"

"Don't be silly, Marian. You know I have problems with bipolar. This is what you've wanted all along. Aren't you happy I'm going to be taking medicine?"

"It doesn't really matter, Sam. It's too late for you to be worrying about how I feel."

They sat in silence while Sam stared at her with an expression she had never seen before. Disregarding the sign on the wall,

—NO PHYSICAL CONTACT—

Sam reached over and took hold of Marian's hand while giving her a provocative wink. As soon as the guard in the room was distracted by another prisoner, Sam saw his chance. He quickly grabbed Marian and hugged her tight. Breathing hard with pleasure and anticipation, he kissed her. In all her life, Marian had never despised anyone as much as she despised Sam at that very moment. She jerked away from him, quickly drawing her sleeve across her mouth in disgust.

He was outraged. "What good are you to me now? Huh, Marian? Answer me! What good are you to me now?"

Marian walked away without looking back.

—Chapter 13—

THE GROUP

SAM WAS ALLOWED ONE CALL EACH WEEK. Marian reluctantly picked up the phone, her stomach in knots at the thought of talking to him. They needed to discuss some urgent business matters.

"Sam, the mortgage hasn't been paid, and you closed our savings account. What did you do with all of the money we had in that account?"

Sam became defensive. "Well, it was my money."

"No, Sam, it was our money. What did you do with it?"

"This isn't the time to talk about the past, Marian. Just drop it."

Marian was undaunted by Sam's attitude as she continued her questioning. "I saw the personal ad you put in the paper. You said you were looking for a soul-mate. I thought I was your soul-mate. Just how many soul-mates do you need, Sam?" Her voice was loud and sarcastic.

"I ... I'm sorry," Sam answered quietly.

Marian was unimpressed by his apology. "Sam, we're losing the house because I can't pay the mortgage, and the kids are worried sick about you. All because you refused to take a little pill ... a god-damn little pill, Sam. That's all it would have taken and we could have had a great life."

Marian didn't wait for him to answer. She slammed the phone down in disgust. She knew she had no choice ... the house had to be sold.

"Paint the dining room, shampoo the rugs, call the realtor," she noted as she walked from room to room. Memories of her life with Sam came flooding over her. There had been some wonderful times in this house, but there had also been a lot of heartache. At that moment, she could only feel a great deal of sorrow building within her.

On her next visit to the prison, Marian told Sam about the minor repairs she was making to the house and told him about her meeting with the realtor.

"Are you upset that the house is for sale, Sam?"

"No, there are lots of other houses. We can start over when I get out of here. As long as I have you, everything will be fine."

Marian was struck by what Sam had just said. Even though it had only been a few months, he seemed to have forgotten the desperate and demented state he had been in and the irreparable damage it had caused.

Marian, however, couldn't just forget about the consequences of Sam's behavior. She had to take care of so many things: selling the house, finding a new place to live, getting a job so she could pay her bills. She felt overwhelmed by the list of responsibilities.

One afternoon, Marian decided it was time to do something nice for herself. She had some books to return to the library and thought the walk would help clear her head. The fresh air was invigorating as Marian walked as far as the park. She found an empty bench near the children's playground and sat down to rest. She watched intently as two little boys chased each other, whooping and hollering with glee. It lightened her mood to see how carefree they were. She soaked up the warm sun and noticed how blue the sky was.

"Maybe life isn't so bad after all," she concluded as she slowly continued her walk.

As Marian entered the library, something caught her eye. Just inside the door, she saw a long table covered with pamphlets. On the wall above the table was a sign:

—FREE INFORMATION FROM THE—
NATIONAL ALLIANCE FOR THE MENTALLY ILL

Marian grabbed a brochure and headed for the nearest chair. She quickly scanned the information until she saw the time and place of the organization's next meeting. She had never been overly fond of support groups, but she thought this might be just the kind of group she needed.

The meeting was held in the home of one of the members. Marian was nervous as she knocked on the door. A polite young man welcomed her and led her into a spacious living room. As Marian walked in, she saw people chatting amiably as they munched on snacks. Everyone greeted her warmly, and a pleasant-looking older woman in her 70's patted the sofa beside her. "Come sit here. There's plenty of room." Marian took a cookie and a cup of coffee with her and settled beside the woman.

Soon the meeting began. People introduced themselves and told brief histories about the mental illnesses of their loved ones. Marian began to feel less alone as she listened to their stories. Finally it was her turn to speak. She talked rapidly, hoping to get through Sam's story before she lost her courage. She told about her life with Sam and of all the unsettling events of the past few months. Everyone sat and listened intently. No one looked surprised, no one gasped, no one tried to tell her what to do. Instead, they listened patiently as she poured out the sordid details.

When Marian finally finished speaking, she felt her face redden. She looked down at the floor, feeling embarrassed that she had taken so much of their time. When a distinguished-looking gentleman near her began to talk, she glanced up at his kind face.

"We understand how difficult this has been for you, Marian. We're here to help in any way we can. Now, do you have any questions you would like to ask us?"

Marian's eyes began to fill with tears.

"Sam says he will go back on his medicine and then everything will be okay. But how do I know that this time will be different? We've been down this road so many times before. Should I stay with him?"

Marian knew there wasn't one 'right' answer to her question, so she wasn't surprised at the advice the group gave her.

"Marian, we have experienced many of the same problems you're dealing with, so we understand this is such a difficult decision for you to make. Give yourself some time. In your heart, you will know what is best for you … and for Sam."

As the meeting ended, Marian felt comforted. She was surrounded by warm, caring people and felt buoyed by their strength. As she headed toward the door, she heard a chorus of voices: "Bye, Marian … Glad you came … Here is some information for you to read … Hang in there … Hope to see you at our next meeting." On her drive home, she thought of the wonderful people she had met. She was already looking forward to the next meeting.

When she got out of bed the next morning, Marian felt energized. After a quick breakfast, she walked to the garage and opened the large overhead door. Facing her were the stacks of boxes Sam had stored there after the garage sale. She couldn't avoid this job any longer ... it was time for her to get busy. As she looked at the items in each box, she had to make some hard decisions: what to keep, what to give to the kids, what to take to the curb for garbage pick-up. All of the items had value ... maybe not in dollars and cents, but certainly in the memories they had created during her years with Sam.

She leaned against the wall of the garage, looking at the assortment of items. Angry tears formed. "Damn him," she muttered. "Doesn't he think about all the years we spent here, the Christmases and birthdays we celebrated? Doesn't he remember the family get-togethers, or the great times we had when friends came to visit? How could he throw all that away?"

As she continued going through the boxes, she thought about Sam's kids. Marian was thankful she had a strong relationship with Samantha and George. Whether she stayed with Sam or not, she was sure the two of them would continue to be an important part of her life.

After a long morning of sorting and tossing, Marian took a break. She grabbed a soda and sat down in her favorite spot: the front stoop. For some reason, she always did her best thinking there. The many decisions she needed to make were weighing heavily on her mind.

She recalled her recent conversation with all the kids. She told them she wasn't sure what, if any, future she would have with Sam. They had reassured her. "Do what you need to do for yourself. We'll be here for you no matter what you decide."

"What great kids they are," she told herself. She was so proud of them.

Now that Sam was back on his medicine, his moods had begun to stabilize. During her most recent visit with him, she had seen glimpses of the 'old Sam'. As Marian sipped her soda, she recalled a question he had asked her. "Are you going to leave me, Marian?"

She had given him an honest answer. "Sam, that is a possibility."

—Chapter 14—

Is The Roller Coaster Ride Over?

When Sam was released from prison, he was transferred to a half-way house. He would be on probation for the next five years, and if he stayed on his medication and followed the rules, he would be able to have a decent life. The house was sold, legal fees and fines were paid, and there were no more loose ends to be handled.

When Marian decided to leave Chicago, she had one last visit with Sam. Although she had done her best to prepare him for this day, he seemed surprised when she told him she was leaving.

She wished him well, gave him a quick hug, and turned to go. Before opening the door, she turned for one last glimpse. As she looked into Sam's sorrowful eyes, a surge of emotion swept over her. Not the love that she once had for Sam. Not the anger she had experienced. Just a profound feeling of sadness.

—The End—

—PART TWO—

PART TWO IS FOR INFORMATIONAL PURPOSES ONLY. It is not meant to be used as a diagnostic tool. It is important that you seek a professional evaluation if you have concerns about yourself or a loved one.

—Chapter 1—

Understanding Bipolar Disorder

BIPOLAR ILLNESS—FORMELY CALLED *MANIC DEPRESSION*— is a mood disorder that causes a person to go through extreme changes in mood, alternating between depression and mania. As the person goes back and forth between these two extremes, we say that the person is cycling. The amount of time between cycles will vary from person to person. Some individuals are rapid cyclers, going from low to high and back again several times a day. Others will go for weeks, possibly even months or years, before cycling to the other extreme.

Bipolar disorder is a form of mental illness that causes severe disturbances in thinking, feeling, and relating, thus hindering a person's ability to cope with the ordinary demands of life. Approximately 3% of adults in the United States have bipolar disorder. It affects men and women equally and is found in people of all races and ethnic backgrounds. Results of many studies indicate that there is a strong genetic link. A person who has a close relative with this disorder will be up to three times more likely to be diagnosed as well. People with a history of depression are also at increased risk.

Bipolar disorder is not the same as clinical depression. Because many individuals initially seek treatment for their depressive symptoms, this often leads to an inaccurate diagnosis of depression. In order to be diagnosed with bipolar disorder, there must be periods of mania in addition to the depressive lows. It is important to make the distinction between bipolar disorder and depression in order to receive proper care.

WHAT CAUSES THIS?

Learning how the brain functions is a key to understanding bipolar disorder. The brain is a highly complex organ, sending messages to every part of our body. It is the command center, regulating such things as breathing, memory, speech, emotions, and thinking.

The brain is made up of billions of nerve cells called neurons, each one connected chemically and electrically to the others. These neurons transmit information to each other, sending and receiving messages by chemical and electrical means. This messaging is made possible by chemicals within the brain. These chemicals, called neurotransmitters, help electrical impulses go from one neuron to another. Seratonin, the "feel-good" chemical, is just one of the neurotransmitters directly associated with mental health. If there is an imbalance in these chemicals or a problem with the 'electrical wiring', the neurons are unable to communicate effectively with each other. When this happens, the brain's complex system isn't working properly and health problems—including mental illness—can occur. To put it simply, the brain of a person with bipolar disorder isn't functioning in the same way as that of a person not affected by the disorder.

There is a direct link between the chemical levels in the brain and bipolar disorder. Too much or too little of certain important neurotransmitters disrupts the brain's intricate functioning. Medication is used to bring these chemicals back to a healthy level, thus allowing the neurons to function normally. This, in turn, helps stabilize the mood swings associated with bipolar disorder.

SYMPTOMS

Although symptoms will vary somewhat from person to person, all people with bipolar disorder have some of the following behavioral characteristics:

Changes In Thinking Or In Perceiving Information:
a. Hallucinations
b. Delusional thinking
c. Excessive fears or suspicions

Changes In Mood:
a. Sadness unrelated to events or circumstances
b. Loss of interest in pleasurable activities
c. Thinking or talking about suicide
d. Extreme excitement or euphoria
e. Pessimism
f. Feelings of hopelessness

Changes In Behavior:
a. Abnormal self-involvement
b. Drug or alcohol abuse
c. Inappropriate laughter
d. Inability to concentrate
e. Difficulty coping with minor problems
f. Peculiar use of words

g. Engaging in risky or dangerous activities

h. Bizarre behaviors such as staring, posturing, act
ing strangely.

i. Heightened sensitivity to one's environment

j. Unusual anger

Physical Changes:

a. Hyperactivity or inactivity

b. Deterioration in hygiene and personal care

c. Unexplained weight gain or loss

d. Excessive sleeping or being unable to sleep

e. pressured speech or a lack of response

While a single symptom or isolated event is not necessarily a cause for alarm, multiple or severe symptoms indicate
a need for medical evaluation.

THE CYCLE OF DEPRESSION

The depression referred to in this book is not just a tempo-
rary case of the blues, an occasional bad mood, or the ups
and downs all of us experience as a part of daily life. Instead,
it is the bipolar type of depression: a serious medical condition that alters the way a person feels, thinks, and acts. It
robs an individual of all energy and joy, leaving overwhelming sadness and hopelessness in its place. A person with depression can't just pull himself up by the bootstraps or simply get over it. Instead, it is an illness that wreaks havoc on
every part of a person's life.

The depressed person will have low energy levels, and
in some cases, may have difficulty getting out of bed each
morning. He will feel sad and dejected, and may have bouts

of crying. A depressed person also has difficulty concentrating and is easily distracted. Making even the smallest decisions can be almost impossible. It is common for the depressed person to lose interest in normal daily activities, and he will often isolate himself from the important people in his life. He may be unable to properly care for himself, forgetting to eat, bathe, or take daily medication.

Depression makes everyday life very difficult. Some describe depression as being in a dark tunnel with no light at the end. Others talk about the feeling of being stuck in quicksand or of having to drag around what feels like heavy chains. Some may contemplate suicide as a way of getting relief from the deep dark hole of depression.

Depression affects people of all ages, races, religions, and sexual orientations. It has touched the lives of many famous people: Vincent Van Gogh, Abraham Lincoln, Marilyn Monroe, John Lennon, and Mike Wallace are just a few of the well-known people who have dealt with depression.

THE CYCLE OF MANIA

Just as depression causes a person to live in a world of slow motion, the cycle of mania creates a life of excess and passion. As a person cycles from depression into mania, he will experience an elevated mood and high energy. Delusional thinking, compulsive urges, and obsessive behaviors are also typical.

The individual with mania will have a decreased need for sleep along with a marked increase in energy. He will experience racing and disconnected thoughts, it will be difficult for him to concentrate, and his speech may be unusually rapid and loud.

It is also common for a person with bipolar mania to spend excessive amounts of money: going on wild shopping sprees and making extravagant purchases. At times, the person may feel invincible and have delusions of grandeur, believing he has special god-like powers and abilities. He may engage in risky behaviors, such as driving recklessly or participating in dangerous activities. The person in a manic cycle may also have increased sexual energy and participate in inappropriate sexual behavior.

When a person is manic, he may become overly aggressive or violent. This can lead to verbal or physical assaults. There may also be times when the person has paranoid or psychotic thoughts.

Being in a manic state is like driving 75 MPH in a 35 MPH zone. In fact, mania used to be a non-specific term for madness because of the frenetic thoughts and behaviors associated with it.

SUICIDE

People with bipolar disorder are at a high risk for suicide, especially if the person is not in treatment. Although statistics vary, most experts agree that at least 25% of those with this disorder will attempt suicide at some point in their lives.

SOME OF THE WARNING SIGNS FOR SUICIDE ARE:

1. Talking about harming oneself or about death.
2. Taking care of personal business, updating wills, check ing insurance policies.
3. Giving away prized possessions.
4. Making comments such as "It would be better if I wasn't around" or "I'm tired of being a burden."

5. Acting or driving recklessly, as though there was a "death wish."
6. A change from being very depressed to being calm and peaceful.

If you notice that a loved one is exhibiting suicidal thoughts or behaviors, recognize that this is a serious situation. Talk openly with the person about your concerns. There is a common misconception that if a person talks about suicide, he won't actually follow through. This is not true! Ask the person if he has a plan for harming himself. Take all comments seriously, even if they seem far-fetched or illogical.

If you feel that a suicide attempt is imminent, remove anything the person may use to harm himself, such as guns, knives, or pills. Do not leave the person alone. Above all, seek help immediately, even if the person resists.

Ironically, many people commit suicide just as they begin to feel better. When a person is in a depressed state, he is likely to be too passive and overwhelmed to take any action. As the energy level and depressed feelings begin to improve, however, the person may be more likely to carry out a suicide plan. Continue to be vigilant even though you see a lessening of the depression.

A few people with bipolar disorder also have periods of time when depression and mania exist at the same time. This is called a 'mixed state'. The impulsiveness of mania co-mingles with the feelings of hopelessness, leaving the person especially vulnerable to suicide.

If you notice any warning signs, do not be afraid to talk to your loved one about the risk of suicide. You will not be putting the idea into his head. People who have suicidal thoughts don't want to die—they just want to stop the emotional pain and anguish. Remind them that suicide is a long-term solution to a short-term problem.

TREATMENT OPTIONS

It is important to remember that bipolar disorder is a medical illness. Anyone with bipolar symptoms should be under the care of a reputable medical doctor. There are various treatments available to help a person lead a more stable life. The management of this illness is a lifelong process, and there may be some 'trial and error' involved in finding the most effective treatment options.

Medication is usually the first thing a doctor will recommend. This stabilizes the mood swings and helps restore a balance of chemicals in the brain. Lithium is the one most commonly prescribed, but it is not unusual for a doctor to recommend a combination of medications. Because each person responds differently, it may be necessary to try different medications in order to find the most effective one. It is very important to work closely with the doctor in order to gauge the effectiveness of the medication and to monitor possible side effects. The doctor will also have the latest information on new drugs that are available to treat this disorder.

Therapy is often used in conjunction with medication. The therapist can help the person accept the diagnosis and gain a better understanding of the illness. When a person begins treatment for bipolar disorder, it is common for him to miss the exuberance and elevated mood that accompany mania. The therapist can help the person understand the destructive nature of mania and the importance of controlling the mood swings.

In addition, therapy can help the person develop coping strategies to assist with daily living, and can aid in minimizing stress. Therapy also helps the individual understand the ways in which his illness affects his interactions with family and friends. This disorder can strain even the strongest relationships, so including loved ones in some therapy sessions can sometimes be helpful.

Herbal and natural supplements such as St. John's Wort or Omega 3 fatty acids seem to help some people. Researchers are not sure why these products help some individuals or how they may interact with other medications the person may be taking. It is important to let the doctor know if these supplements are being used.

If the depressive cycle is quite severe or if medication hasn't been effective, some people may benefit from electroconvulsive therapy (ECT). Electrical currents are sent through the brain, triggering a small seizure. This causes a change in the electro-chemical processes of the brain, thus alleviating some of the bipolar symptoms. It is a controversial treatment and is usually used only in cases where the person hasn't responded well to any other treatments.

In situations where the person is a threat to himself or to others, hospitalization may be necessary. Psychotic thinking, acute manic behavior, talk of suicide, or threats against others are indications that the person needs to be hospitalized.

—Chapter 2—

Bipolar Children and Adolescents

Researchers, such as the renowned Emil Kraepelin, have explored the subject of bipolar disorder as early as the turn of the century. However, it has only been since the mid-90's that any significant research has been done to determine if this disorder can also affect children. Now, with our greater understanding of the brain and its role in mental illness, the National Institute of Mental Health has stated that bipolar disorder can, in fact, affect children as well as adults.

It can be difficult to diagnose this disorder in children, however. The symptoms of bipolar disorder can be easily confused with those of other problems such as attention-deficit-hyperactive disorder, obsessive-compulsive disorder, panic disorder, or substance abuse. For this reason, misdiagnosis can frequently occur.

When this disorder occurs in a child, it causes cognitive and behavioral problems just as the child is undergoing crucial development and learning. For that reason, early intervention is very important. Parents should seek the help of professionals specially trained in the care of children and adolescents. A child psychiatrist is preferable, but if one is not available, parents should consult a pediatric neurologist or a psychiatrist who specializes in mood disorders.

Medication and therapy are the standard treatments for children with bipolar disorder. It is imperative that parents maintain a close relationship with their child's doctor as a treatment regimen is developed. Because children's bodies metabolize medications differently than adult bodies, it is important to monitor the effectiveness of the medications as well as to watch for any potential side-effects. The dosages will also need to be adjusted as the child grows.

Along with medication, therapy can be beneficial. This will provide a supportive environment as the child learns to live with bipolar disorder. Therapy, along with medication, can provide the stability a child needs to lead a happy and productive life.

LITHIUM—The old standby; eases symptoms by regulating several neurotransmitters, but doesn't work for everyone

ANTICONVULSANT DRUGS—First used for epilepsy, such medications as Depakote and Lamictal calm manic storms

ATYPICAL ANTIPSYCHOTICS—Drugs designed to help schizophrenics battle delusions, including Zyprexa and Risperdal, can do the same for bipolar

ANTIDEPRESSANTS—Risky, since they can trigger bipolar cycling, but drugs such as Prozac may be part of the mix

LIFESTYLE—Schedules are key, with fixed bed and wake-up times. Foods with caffeine would be limited. Teens should avoid drugs and alcohol

INDIVIDUAL THERAPY—Kids need counseling to help them balance sleep, meals, work and play. They also must talk about problems at home and resolve crises that can trigger the disorder.

FAMILY THERAPY—Parents must learn when to give in to a child-this is critical early in treatment-and when to stay firm. Family bickering should be kept to a minimum. Siblings can serve as trusted eyes and ears for a child whose perceptions are out of whack.

—Chapter 3—

Symptoms Of Psychiatric Illness

AGITATION

Restlessness, wringing of hands, pacing the floor, rubbing and picking at skin, excessive worrying and complaining.

Try to remove person from the cause of agitation. Prevent family member from injuring themself. Try to divert his attention to pleasurable activities.

AMNESIA

Loss of memory for past events and/or people.

Protect family member from embarrassment by only talking about things they can clearly remember.

ANXIETY

A strong feeling of fear and uncertainty.

Provide encouragement in a calm and reassuring way. If possible, remove the cause of of anxiety, and protect them from any suicide attempts.

APATHY

A feeling of indifference: a blank mood.

Stimulate their interest and mood with a cheerful, bright environment. Talk with enthusiasm, and encourage their participation in interesting activities.

BELLIGERENCE AGGRESSION
Arguing, threatening, fighting, wanting to start arguments.

Do not become aggressive yourself. Stay as calm as possible and avoid topics or situations that may annoy them. Do not argue or attempt to reason with them. If the situation is threatening, leave immediately.

BIZZARE BEHAVIOR
Acting strangely, dressing or behaving in unusual ways.

Do not appear disgusted or laugh about unusual behaviors or choice of clothing. Gently point out that they are acting or dressing in a manner that may illicit negative responses from others.

COMPULSION
An irresistible urge to act or behave in a way the person seems unable to control.

Do not ridicule them or make fun of them. Reassure them that it is not essential to engage in the compulsive behavior, and try to divert his attention away from the behavior.

CONFABULATION
Giving fictitious accounts of the past in order to cover up the effects of amnesia.

Gently remind them of details about past events and people. Don't scold or laugh at the stories. They are not altering the past in order to be deceitful.

DELUSIONS
False beliefs which persist even when contradicted by evidence and reasoning.

Do not argue or point blame, On the other hand, do not say or do anything to make them feel that the delusion is true. Calmly state the truth, and inform his doctor about the delusional thinking.

DEPRESSION
A strong feeling of sadness and hopelessness

Gently encourage and support them. Go with them to doctors' appointments, encourage participation in everyday, activities, and assist with daily routines if necessary. Watch closely for any suicidal symptoms, and NEVER say "pull yourself up by the bootstraps" or to "just get over it".

DISORIENTATION
Confusion about who or where you are, what day it is, or a general feeling of confusion about your surroundings.

Calmly give information that they are unsure about. Call them by name, explain where they are, or say the day and month to ease confusion.

DISTRACTABILITY
Difficulty with concentration; noticing every sound and motion that makes it difficult to focus.

Keep the environment as calm and quiet as possible. When talking, say their name and wait for them to look at you before starting your conversation. Keep the radio and TV turned off when concentration is needed.

EROTIC BEHAVIOR
Unusual preoccupation with sexual thoughts and behavior

Do not appear shocked or disgusted by sexual things that they do. Act firmly and matter-of-factly when dealing with interest in sexual matters. Make sure he does not expose himself or make advances toward others.

EUPHORIA
Excessive happiness and elation without real cause

Thoughts jump rapidly from one subject to another; no continuity in conversation. Remain calm and quiet when dealing with them. Do not create additional stimuli that will further excite them.

FLIGHT OF IDEAS
Thoughts jump rapidly from one subject to another; no continuity in conversation

Help them stay focused and remind them what they started to talk about. Limit your conversations to one topic, and keep distractions in the environment to a minimum.

GRANDIOSE DELUSION
A delusion in which the person believes he is famous, possesses special abilities, or has great wealth.

Do not go along with the delusion of their special abilities or fame. Call them by their real name and treat normally. Do not pretend that they are, in fact, the person their delusion makes him believe they are.

HALLUCINATIONS
Imaginary sounds, sights, and smells that have no basis in reality, such as hearing voices, seeing things that don't exist,

feeling things crawling on oneself.

Do not pretend you also see or hear the imaginary they tell you about. Avoid arguing about what is "real". Protect them from injuring themself if voices or imaginary people tell them to do dangerous or hurtful things.

HOARDING
Collects or hides excessive quantities of items.

Try to do regular housekeeping to keep excess items from accumulating. Explain the health dangers of hoarding food or of stockpiling items that prevent easy access to other rooms or outdoor exits. Provide adequate space for them to keep valuable belongings, but maintain a sense of order in the rest of the house.

HYPERACTIVITY
Unusually high level of activity and energy; restless and has difficulty concentrating

Keep things as calm as possible. Ensure adequate rest and regular meals. Encourage quiet activities.

INCOHERANCE
Unable to express thoughts in a clear, logical way.

Talk to him as though you expect them to communicate clearly. Watch for body language and facial expressions for clues about what they are trying to say.

INSECURITY
Feeling vulnerable and uneasy; lacking in self-confidence

Respond with empathy and interest, letting them know that you care about their feelings and concerns. Let them know that you sincerely care, and build self-confidence with honest praise and encouragement.

INSTABILITY
Being unstable, unpredictable, or erratic.

Maintain a regular routine and avoid sudden changes or surprises. Try to protect from unpredictable situations or from people that will upset them.

NEGATIVISM
Doing the opposite of what is expected of him, not following instructions, or defying authority

Politely ask for cooperation: do not demand or order to do something. Be specific about what you expect, and give clear-cut suggestions. Keep instructions simple and give opportunity to make small decisions on their own.

PANIC
Debilitating feeling of' anxiety or fear; an overwhelming sense of dread or a sense of danger

Keep the environment as soothing and calm as possible, and provide lots of reassurance and support. Watch for any rash or sudden acts which may cause injury: remain vigilant for as long as the panic lasts.

PHOBIAS
A fear or dislike of something that does not have a rational basis

Listen to expressions of fear or dislike in a non-judgmental way. Don't minimize their feelings or try to convince their fears are unfounded.

PREOCCUPATION
Lost in thought; completely absorbed in something to such an extent that other things are neglected or ignored.

Avoid suddenly interrupting or startling them while deep in thought. Let them know in advance that you will be needing undivided attention; then give a few minutes to finish their activity or thoughts.

SECLUSION
Removing oneself from other people and activities; wanting `to be alone; isolating oneself.

Encourage spending time with the family and to participate in routine daily activities. Do not insist; instead, rely on gentle encouragement. Find activities that have been pleasurable in the past, and invite participation. Try to engage in simple, non-threatening conversations and activities.

SELF-DEPRECATION
Being self-critical; feeling unworthy and unable to do anything right

Ask them to do those things that can be completed successfully. Provide lots of encouragement and build confidence by offering sincere praise for jobs well done.

STUPOR (OR CATATONIC STATE)
A dazed or trance-like state; a lack of awareness of one's ` surroundings

Medical intervention is vital. Take them to a medical facility immediately in order to ascertain the cause. Talk to them even if they don't appear to hear you. Act and speak in their presence in the same way you would if they were fully aware.

SUGGESTIBILITY
Easily influenced by the words or actions of other people

Set a good example because they will tend to imitate the behaviors and attitudes of those closest to them. Make use of their suggestibility to guide behavior and activities in a wholesome and beneficial way.

—Chapter 4—

FREQUENTLY ASKED QUESTIONS

Q: My grandfather has bipolar disorder. Does this run in families?

A: Yes, there is a strong genetic link. If a relative has this disorder, you are much more likely to have it as well. If you look at the medical history of your family tree, you will probably see that bipolar disorder has been passed down through the generations.

Q: My spouse is exhibiting signs of bipolar behavior. What should I do?

A: Talk with them, expressing concern about changes in their behavior that you have been noticing. Encourage them to see a doctor, and show your support by offering to go with them to the appointment. If you have noticed that they are having difficulties at work or with other interpersonal relationships, talk about those issues as well. Avoid being confrontational. If you feel frustrated or angry, it may be better to have another relative or a close friend talk with them.

Q: What if my wife won't stay on her medication?

A: This is not a problem just for those with bipolar disorder. Any person who has to take medication for a significant period of time may have trouble with non-compliance. Do not enable them by counting out pills, refilling prescriptions, or asking them each day if they have taken their medicine. The bottom line is this: if a person is determined not to take the medication, there isn't anything you can do. It is important, however, to let your wife's doctor know that she isn't following the prescribed treatment.

Q: How do I find a good doctor?

A: I strongly recommend that you find a psychologist or psychiatrist who specializes in bipolar disorder. Call the American Psychiatric Association or your local National Alliance for the Mentally Ill for names of doctors in your area. I would not recommend using your family doctor or a counselor to treat this disorder. Because of the high rate of misdiagnosis, it is important to find a specialist you can work with.

Q: What should I do if my loved one becomes violent?

A: It is important to watch for signs of escalating aggression, such as yelling, destroying property, hurting pets, or behaving/speaking in a threatening manner. If you notice any warning signs, you MUST leave the residence and call the police. Do not try to reason with them. Logic will not work with a person in the throes of bipolar aggression. Think first of your own safety, and then seek assistance for your loved one. Letting the situation escalate without calling the police can be very dangerous.

If you feel there is any possibility that your loved one may become aggressive or violent, it is important to have a safety plan:

—Keep a packed suitcase in the trunk of your car. Include clothing, medications, and important phone numbers along with other essential items.
—Make arrangements with a friend or family member so you will have a safe place to go.
—Keep extra car/house keys hidden outdoors in an easily accessible place.

It doesn't matter whether you are a spouse, parent, or grandparent ... or how much you are loved. Always remember that a person in a state of manic aggression will see you as "just a thing."

Q: A good friend has been diagnosed with hypomania. What is that and what can I expect from her?

A: Hypomania is a more moderate form of mania. Those experiencing hypomania feel as though they're on top of the world. You may notice that she is more sociable and energized. Your friend will have an exaggerated sense of well-being: appearing animated and full of optimism. She may also be highly productive and creative---full of plans and ideas. These symptoms seem to be positive and beneficial. However, she will be more likely to make impulsive decisions and engage in reckless behavior without taking into account the possible consequences. She may over-estimate her capabilities, taking on too many responsibilities or tasks at the same time.

A person with hypomania seldom seeks treatment in its initial stages because the symptoms seem positive and beneficial. If left untreated, however, this can escalate into more severe mania or depression.

Q: My brother needs hospitalization, but he won't agree to go. What can we do?

A: Unless your brother agrees to go into the hospital under his own free will, your options are limited. Current civil commitment law states that your brother can only be hospitalized against his wishes if he is a danger to himself or to others. In most states, he can only be held for 72 hours without court action. If you feel that your brother may harm either himself or someone else, contact a mental health professional for advice about how to proceed.

When your brother's bipolar disorder is under control, talk with him about developing a plan of action. This plan, in written form, would be implemented in the event of another episode where he is out of control. People with bipolar disorder often do not realize how impaired they are, or blame all their problems on some cause other than their mental illness. For those individuals who are a danger to themselves or to others, the hospital offers protection and security. Hospitalization can also give the family a much-needed break. However, long-term hospital stays are usually not necessary or desirable.

Q: Can children have bipolar disorder?

A: This is an area of controversy with no clear-cut answer. There are other conditions during childhood that may mimic bipolar disorder: ADHD, conduct disorder, and autism, for example. This makes it nearly impossible to definitively diagnose bipolar disorder in a young child. In addition, most psychiatrists do not recommend medication at a young age. As a child matures, there may be other variables that affect a diagnosis of bipolar disorder, such as hormone imbalance or substance abuse. Doctors are more willing, however, to make such a diagnosis and prescribe treatment when a child reaches adolescence.

Q: Is it common for a person with bipolar disorder to have substance abuse problems also?

A: Yes, many experts believe that at least half of the people diagnosed with serious mental illness also have substance abuse problems. An individual may use drugs and/or alcohol to 'self-medicate' in an attempt to ease the symptoms of depression or anxiety. People with bipolar disorder seem to be especially vulnerable to alcohol abuse.

When a person has been diagnosed with both mental illness and substance abuse, this is called a dual diagnosis. Domestic abuse, suicide attempts, and violent behavior are more prevalent among those with this dual diagnosis. For the loved ones of a person dealing with both problems, the stress can be overwhelming. It is important to reach out to mental health professionals for guidance and emotional support.

—Chapter 5—

SUMMARY

BIPOLAR DISORDER IS A LIFELONG CONDITION. For the people affected by this disorder, life will be challenging. There may be episodes of cycling that will cause disruption of family and work relationships. There may also be times of irrational thinking and unacceptable behavior. If you or someone you love is struggling with the exhilarating highs and crushing lows of this illness, there will be many hurdles to overcome.

However, the picture is not bleak. Thanks to improved treatment options and better medications, the future is getting brighter for those with bipolar disorder. Many studies are taking place to increase our understanding of the brain and its relationship to mental illness. This greater knowledge will lead to more effective treatments in the future. The stigma of mental illness is also lessening. Because of the efforts of organizations such as The National Institute of Mental Health, people are being encouraged to have open, honest dialogues about mental disorders.

Although dealing with bipolar disorder can be difficult, it is important to remember that many people who have this illness are leading successful, productive lives. Finding a good doctor, conscientiously following a treatment regimen, and being surrounded by supportive family and friends can go a long way toward assuring a happy and fulfilling life for those with the disorder and those who love them.

JANICE BINGHAM RENCH
860 WORCESTER RD.
FRAMINGHAM, MA 01702

(e-mail)— JBR@janicerench.com
(web site)—http://janicerench.com/
(blog) — http://janicerench.blogspot.com
(Tel.) — 508-309-0948

—Chapter 6—

Manic Genius

In **Touched with Fire**, psychologist Kay Redfield Jamison explores bipolar disorder's link with artistic temperament.

Lord Byron—The poet was "a young man of tumultuous passions," said his tutor. Byron described his mental state as "a chaos of the mind."

Edgar Allen Poe—Alcoholism is common in bipolars and Poe fit the profile. "What made Poe write was what made Poe drink," said a biographer.

Robert Shumann—The son of a bipolar author, the German composer wrote 130 songs in one year. He died in an asylum.

Vincent Van Gogh—He once wrote of his illness, "The weakness increases from generation to generation." Geneticists now suspect that's true.

Virginia Woolf—She filled her pockets with stones and drowned herself. "I have a feeling I shall go mad."

Ernest Hemingway—Born into a family plagued by suicide, the writer haunted by manic enthusiasms and depressions—

shot himself.

CURT COBAIN—Seattle grunge rocker took his band, Nirvana, to the pinnancle with Nevermind (one song: Lithium) but took his life at 27.

—Chapter 7—

GUIDE TO MENTAL HEALTH SERVICES

American Academy of Child and Adolescent Psychiatry
(202) 966-7300

American Psychological Association
(800) 374-2721

Child and Adolescent Bipolar Foundation
(847) 256-8225

Depression and Bipolar Support Alliance
(800) 826-3632

Mental Health America
(800) 969-6642

National Alliance for Research on Schizophrenia and Depression
(800) 829-8289

National Alliance On Mental Illness (NAMI)
(800) 950-6264

National Depressive and Manic Depressive Association
(312) 642-0049

National Institute of Mental Health
(866) 615-6464

Stanley Center for the Innovative Treatment of Bipolar Disorder
(800) 424-7657

—Chapter 8—

GLOSSARY

ANXIETY DISORDER: Any of several mental disorders that are characterized by extreme or maladaptive feelings of tension, fear, or worry.

ATYPICAL DEPRESSION: A form of major depression or dysthymia in which the person is able to cheer up when something good happens, but then sinks back into depression when the positive event has passed.

CYCLOTHYMIA: A mood disorder characterized by cycling between hypomania and relatively mild depressive symptoms. This pattern lasts for at least a year, and any intermittent periods of normal mood last no longer than two months at a time.

DEPRESSION: A feeling of sadness, hopelessness, or apathy that lasts for at least two weeks.

DYSTHYMIA: A mood disorder that involves being either mildly depressed or irritable most of the day. These feelings occur more days than not for 12 months or longer and are associated with other symptoms.

ELECTROCONVULSIVE THERAPY (ECT): A psychiatric treatment in which a small electric current is passed through the brain, causing a small seizure. It is also sometimes known as shock therapy.

HYPOMANIA: A somewhat high, expansive, or irritable mood that lasts for at least 4 days. The mood is more moderate than mania, but is also clearly different from a person's usual mood when not depressed.

MANIA: A psychiatric disorder characterized by excessive physical activity, rapidly changing ideas, and impulsive behavior.

RAPID CYCLING: A form of bipolar disorder in which four or more mood episodes occur within a single year.

SCHIZOAFFECTIVE: A severe form of mental illness in which an episode of either depression or mania occurs at the same time as the symptoms of schizophrenia.

UNIPOLAR DEPRESSION: Another name for major depressive disorder. The term is used to distinguish from depression which occurs within the context of bipolar disorder.

VAGUS NERVE STIMULATION: A treatment in which a small implanted device delivers mild electrical pulses to the vagus nerve. It is currently being tested for use in severe depression.

—Chapter 9—

RECOMENDED READING

LOVING SOMEONE WITH BIPOLAR DISORDER. –*Julie A. Fast*

BIPOLAR DISORDER: A GUIDE FOR PATIENTS. –*Frances Mark Mondimore*

NIGHT FALLS FAST: UNDERSTANDING SUICIDE.–*Kay Jamison*

TOUCHED WITH FIRE: MANIC DEPRESSION ILLNESS AND THE ARTISTIC TEMPERAMENT. –*Kay Jamison*

AN UNQUIET MIND: A Memoir of Moods and Madness. –*Kay R. Jamison*

A DEEPER SHADE OF BLUE: A WOMEN'S GUIDE TO RECOGNIZING AND TREATING DEPRESSION IN HER CHILDBEARING YEARS. –*Rita Nonacs*

THE BIPOLAR SURVIVAL GUIDE: WHAT YOU AND YOUR FAMILY NEED TO KNOW. –*David Miklowitz*

MANIC-DEPRESSIVE ILLNESS. –*Frederick K. Goodwin and Kay R. Jamison*

THE BIPOLAR CHILD: THE DEFINITIVE AND REASSURING GUIDE TO CHILDHOOD'S MISUNDERSTOOD DISORDER. –*Demitri Pa-*

polos, M.D. and Janice Papolos

DARKNESS VISIBLE. *–William Styron*

MATT THE MOODY HERMIT CRAB. *–Caroline McGee*

All books can be purchased at your local bookstore or internet. Local libraries also carry a wide selection of books on bipolar disorder or mental illness.

OTHER BOOKS
By
JANICE BINGHAM RENCH

FEELING SAFE, FEELING STRONG: How to Avoid Sexual Abuse and What to Do If It Happens to You by Susan Neiburg Terkel and Janice E. Rench

Teen Sexuality Decisions and Choices.

OTHER BOOKS
By
JANICE BINGHAM RENCH

Family Violence: How to Recognize and Survive It (Coping with Modern Issues).

UNDERSTANDING SEXUAL IDENTITY: a Book for Gay Teens and Their Friends.